Flowers & Hearts

Coloring Book!

The Light Side!
Volume 1, Advanced

Tamara Kulish

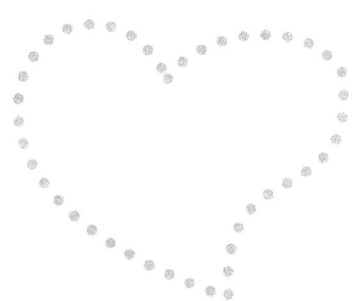

ISBN-13: 978-1717353542
ISBN-10: 1717353541

Published 2018

The Light Side!
Volume 1, Advanced

Flowers and Hearts Coloring book!
Pages and pages of Flowers and Hearts,
all on white backgrounds and
all hand drawn for your coloring pleasure!
These coloring pages are
almost like "Hidden Eye" designs!

For the Coloring book buff! Challenging and Relaxing!

Sit, relax and just have fun!

There's 3-4 challenges for each design,
so your fun is extended!

All of these designs are also on Fine Art America!
http://fineartamerica.com/profiles/tamara-kulish.html
You can order any of their products and
they will custom print and ship it to you!
Imagine painting any one of these designs on a large
pre-printed gallery-wrapped canvas!

Other books available on Tamara's Amazon Author
page:
https://www.amazon.com/Tamara-
Kulish/e/B00IVWCAEI/

Tamara Kulish is an artist, a writer, a
photographer, a jewelry maker,
a seeker and a life voyager.

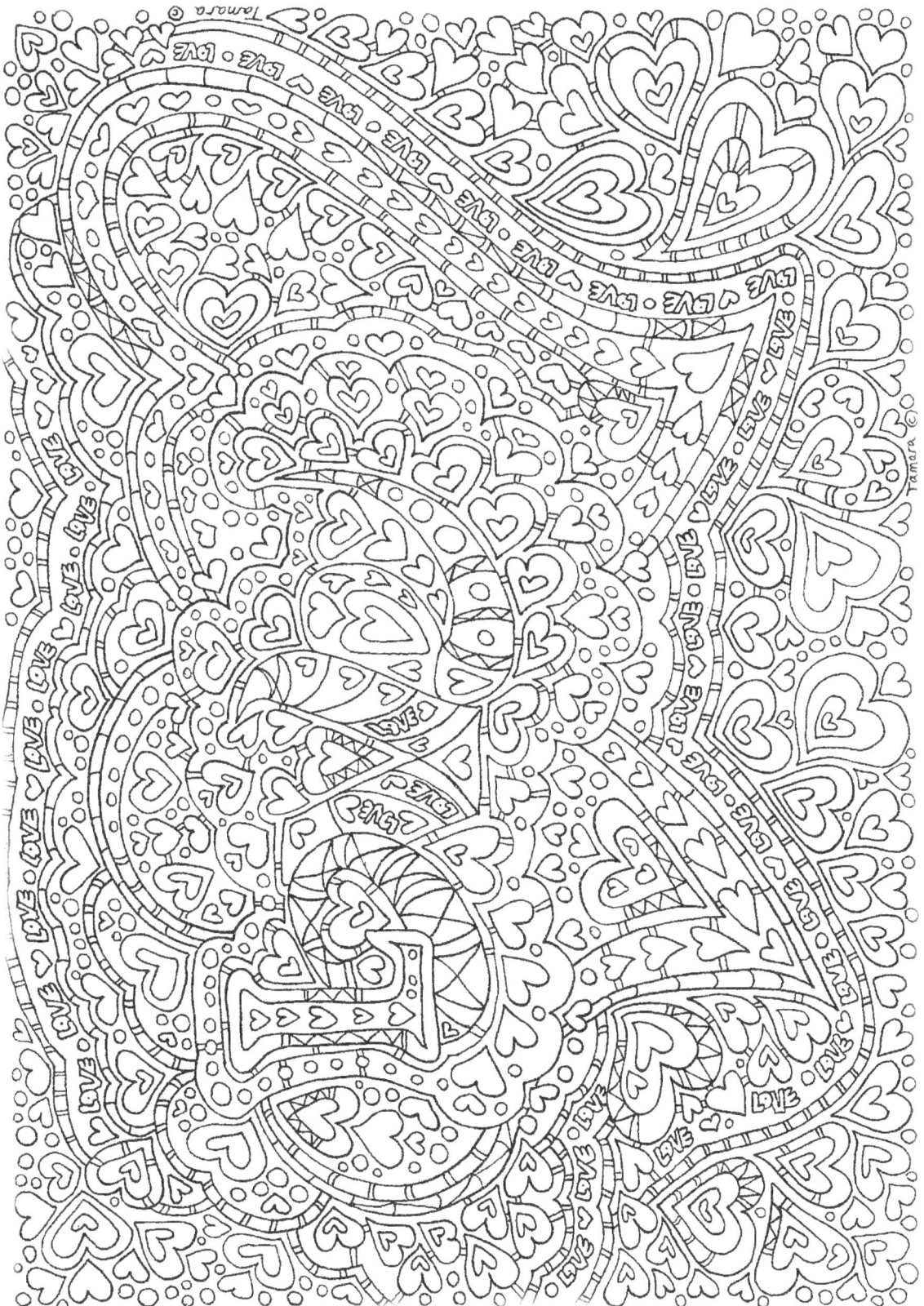

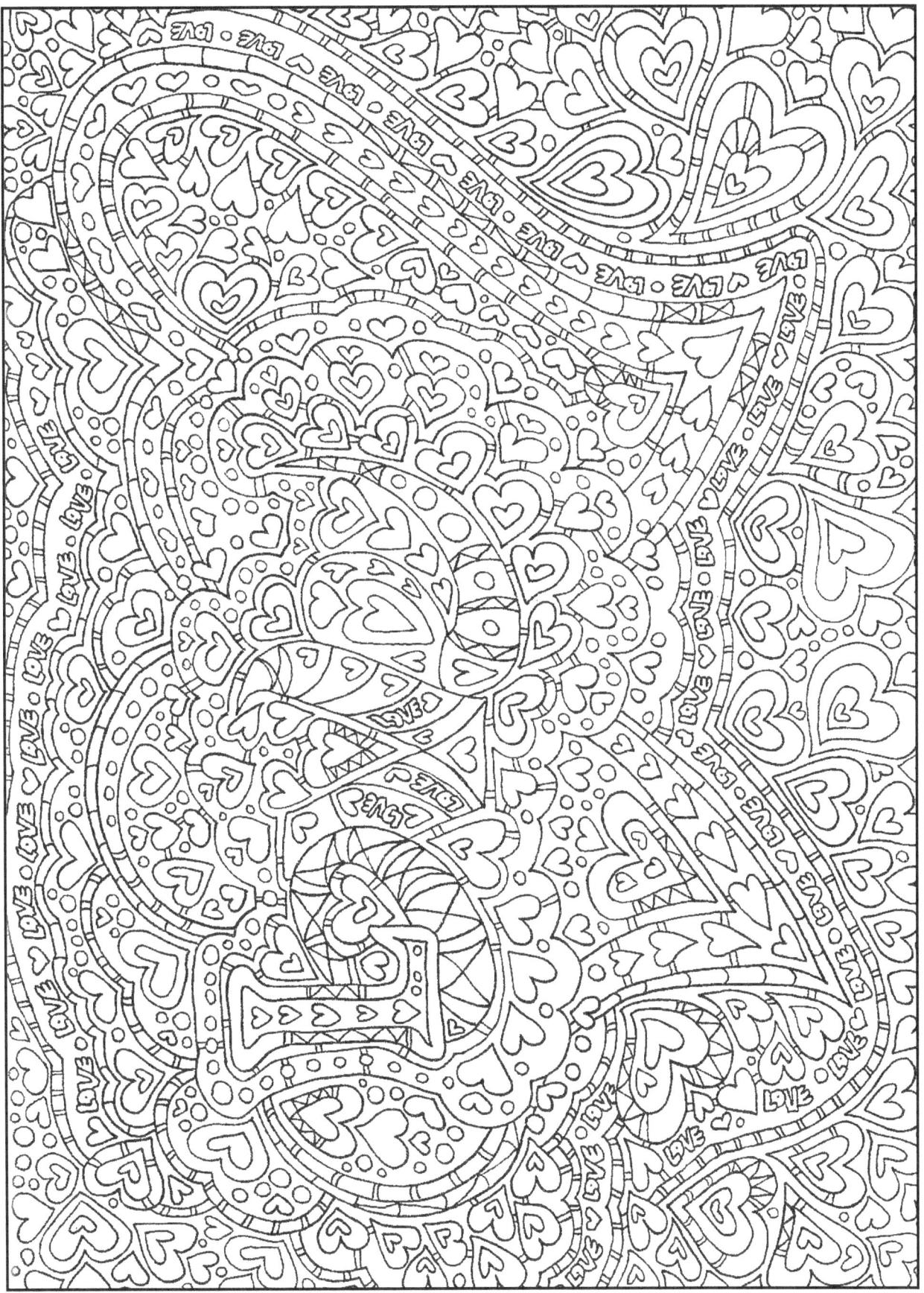

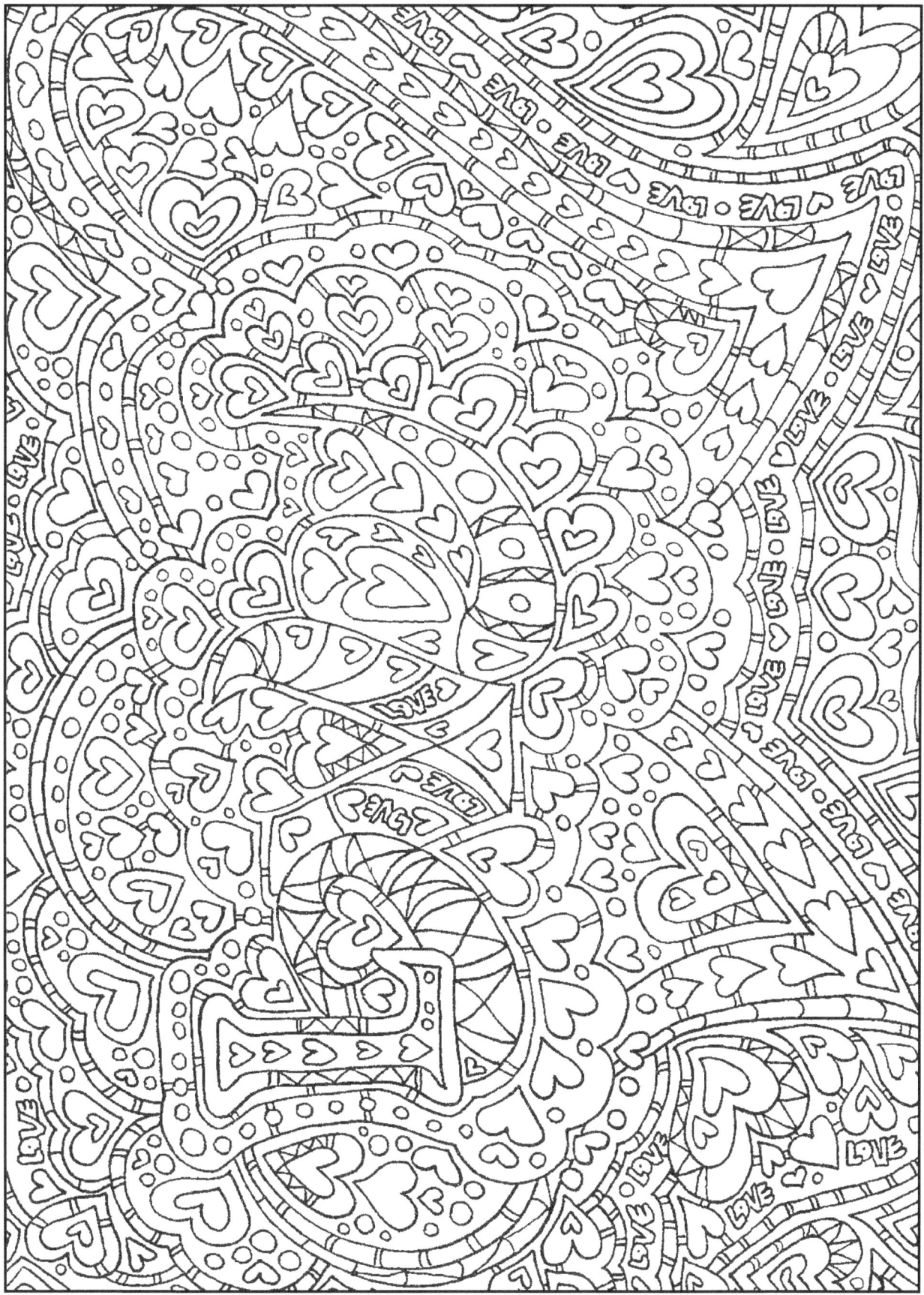

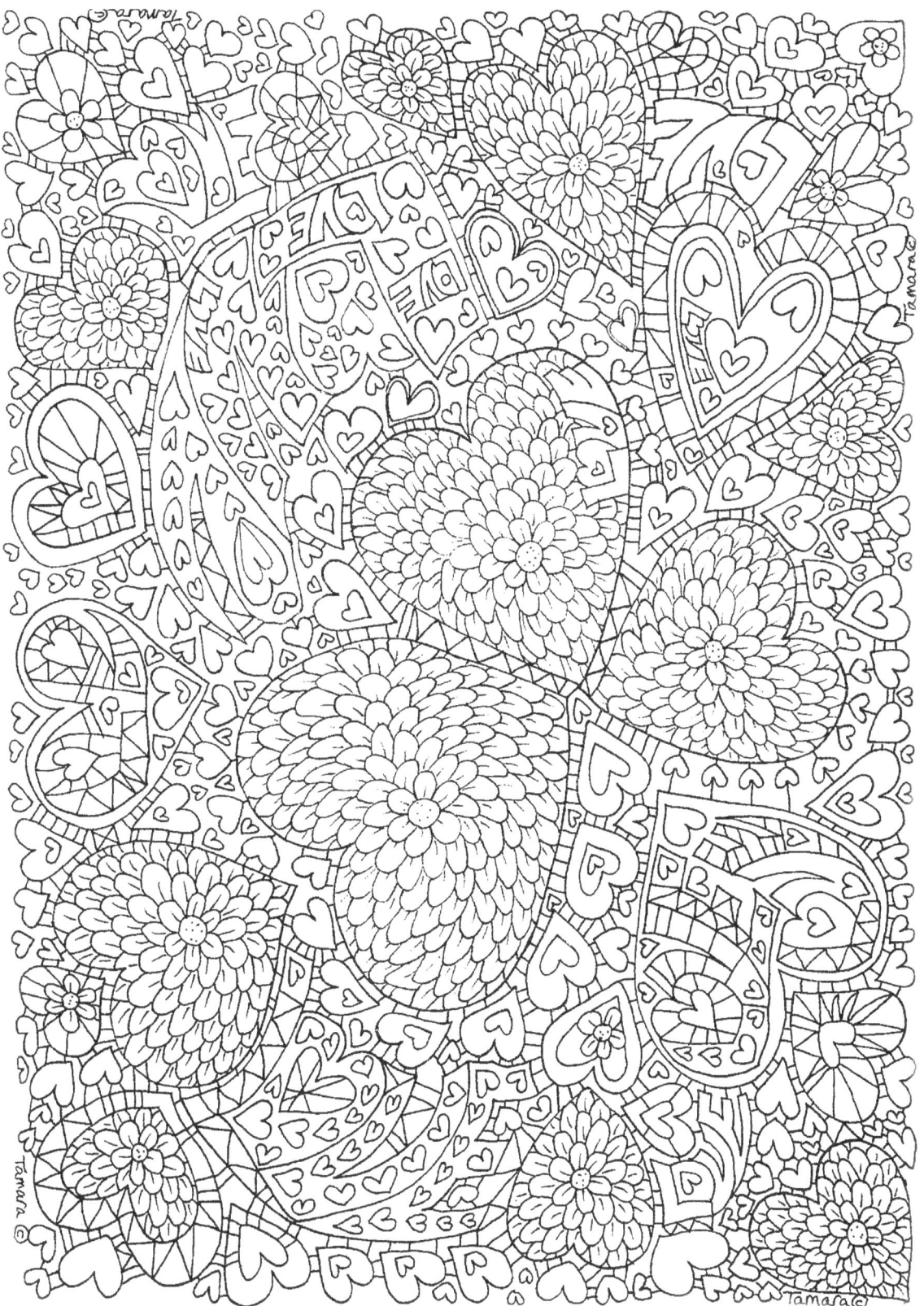

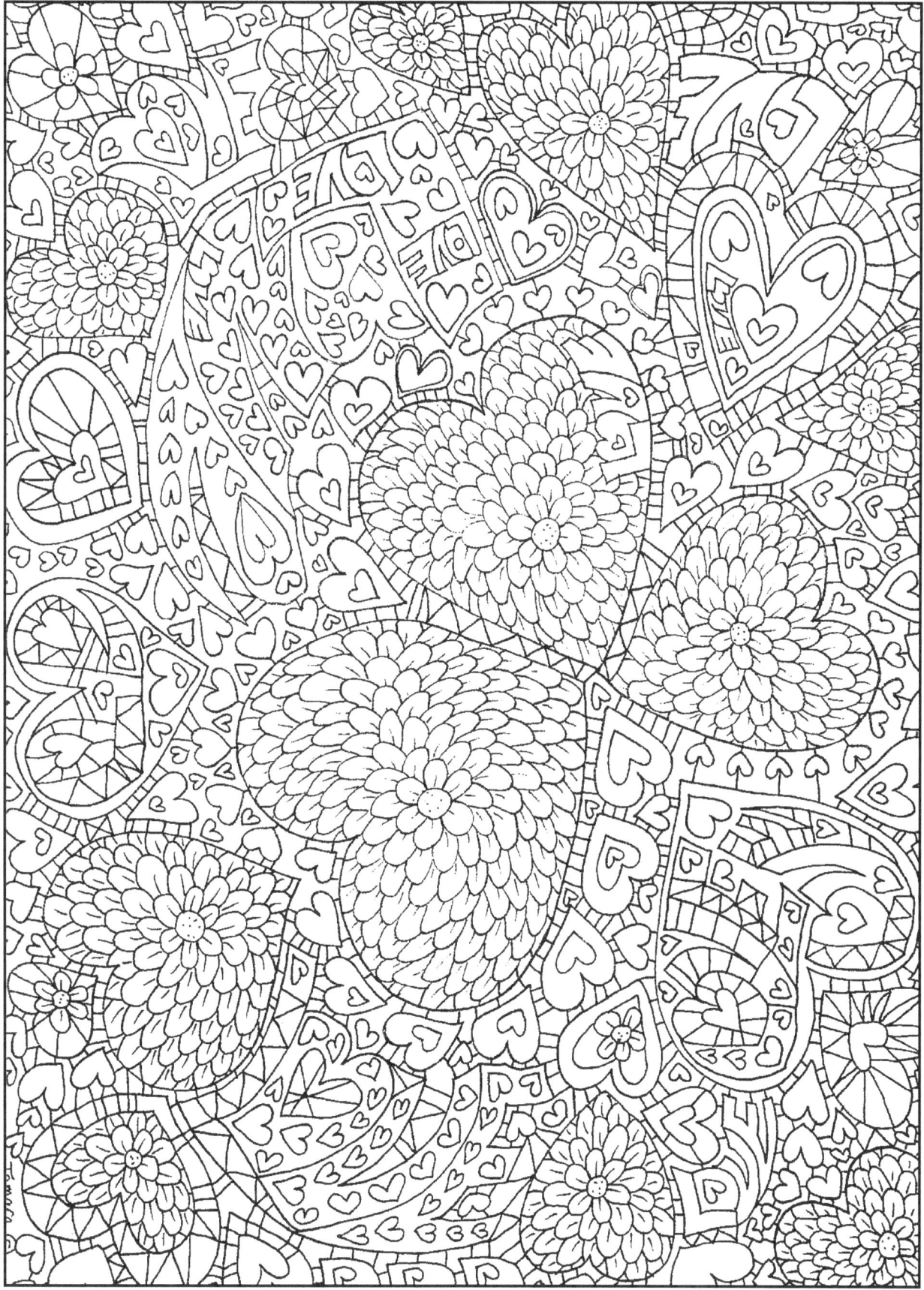

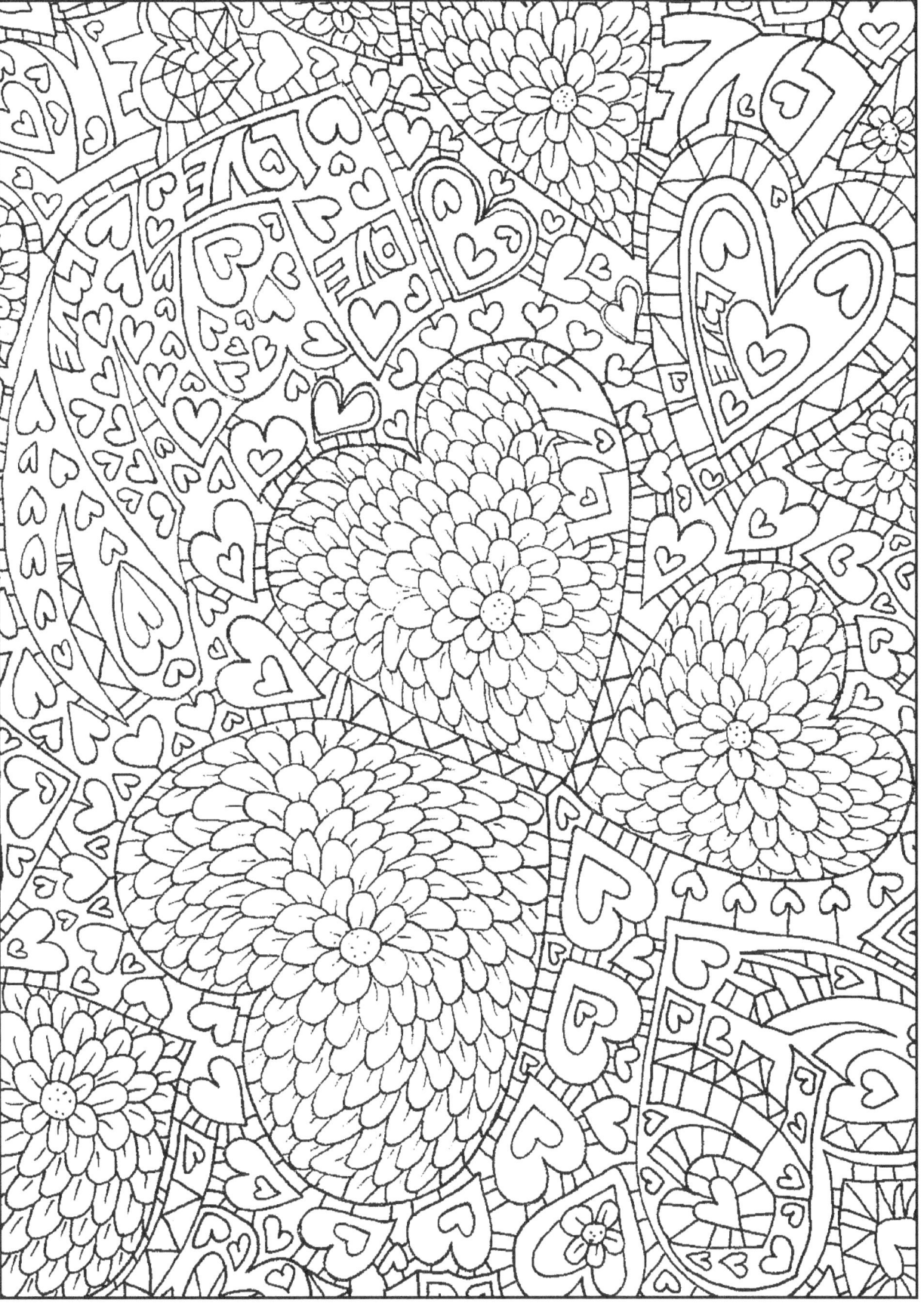

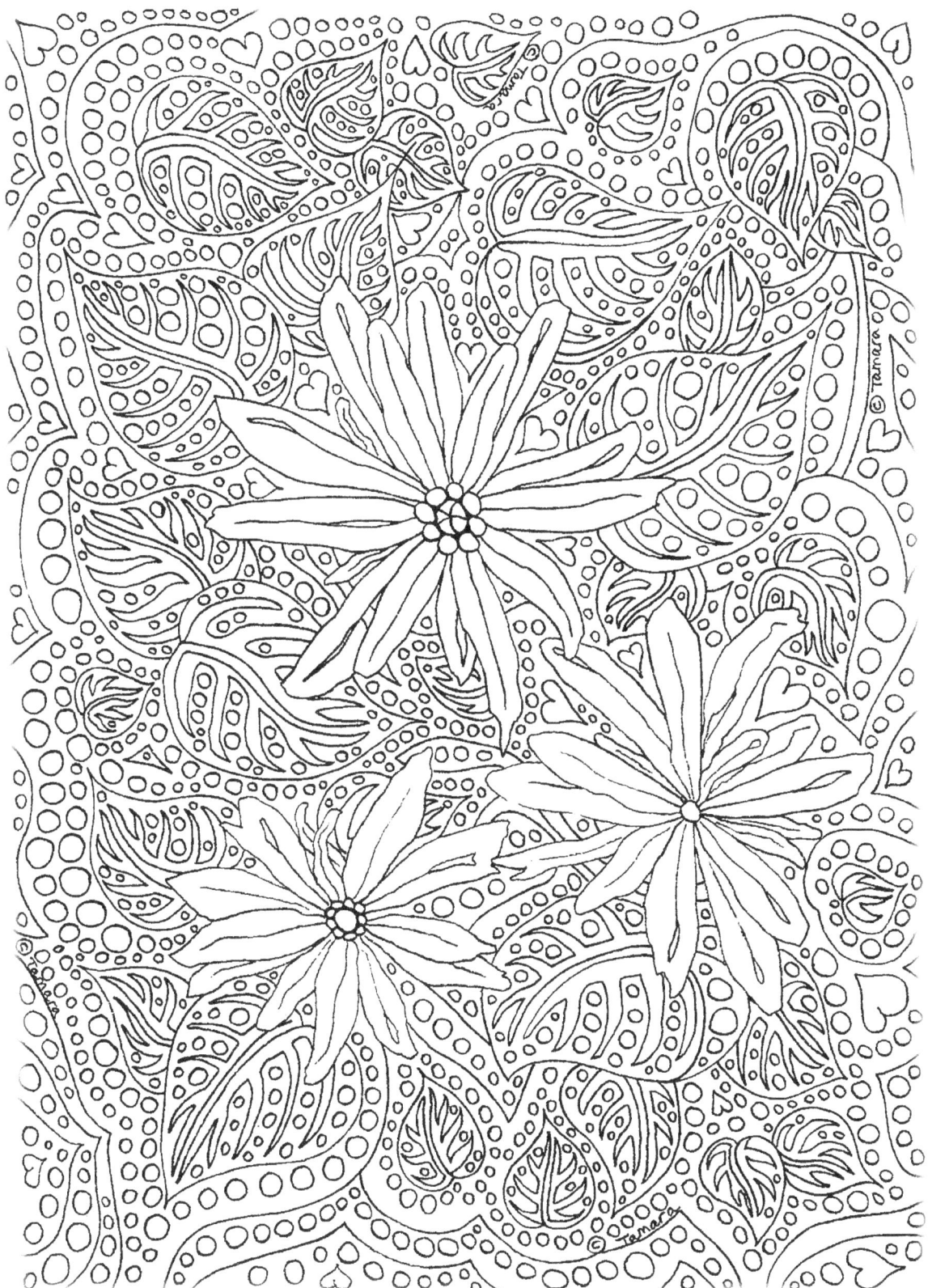

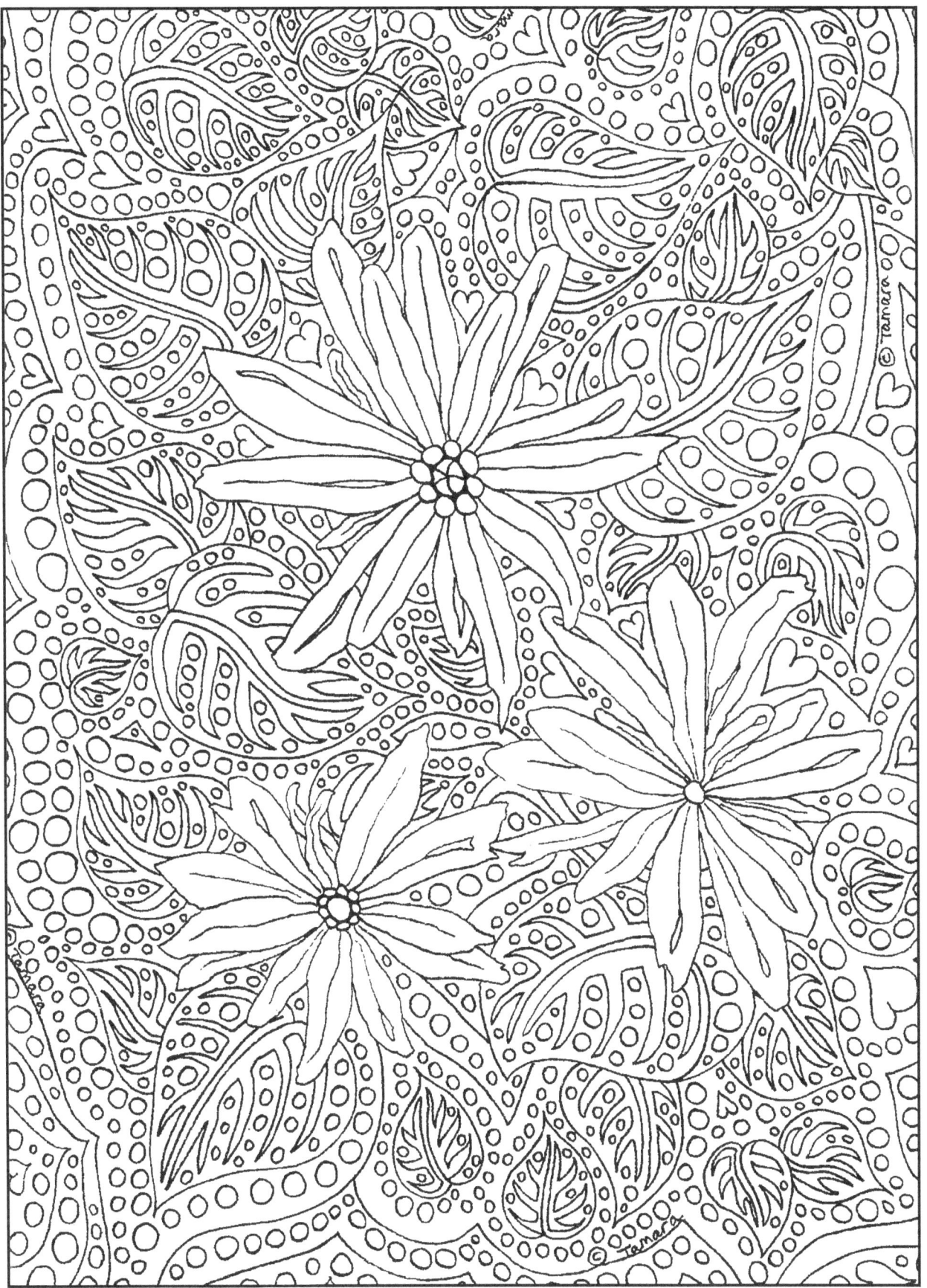

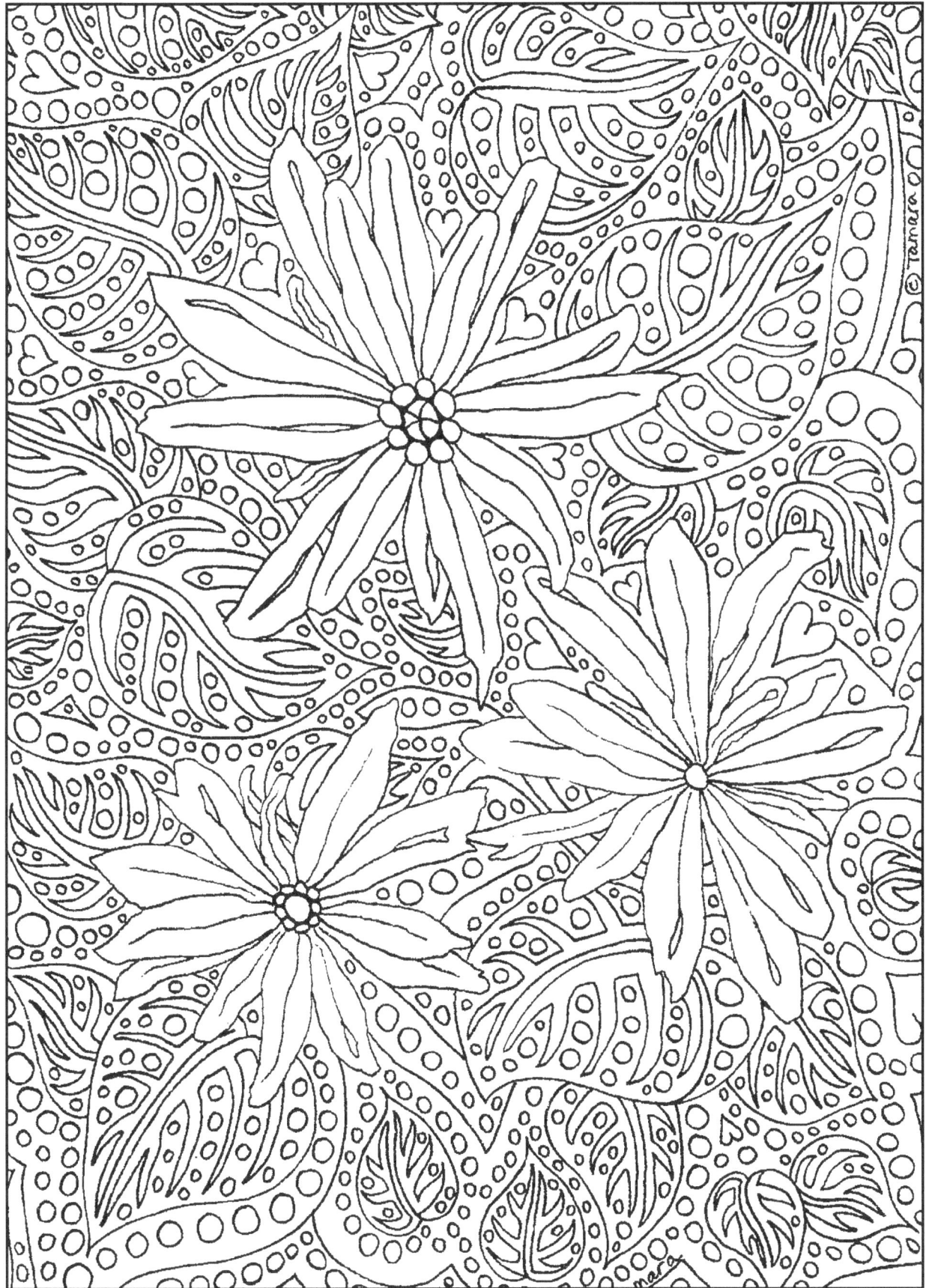

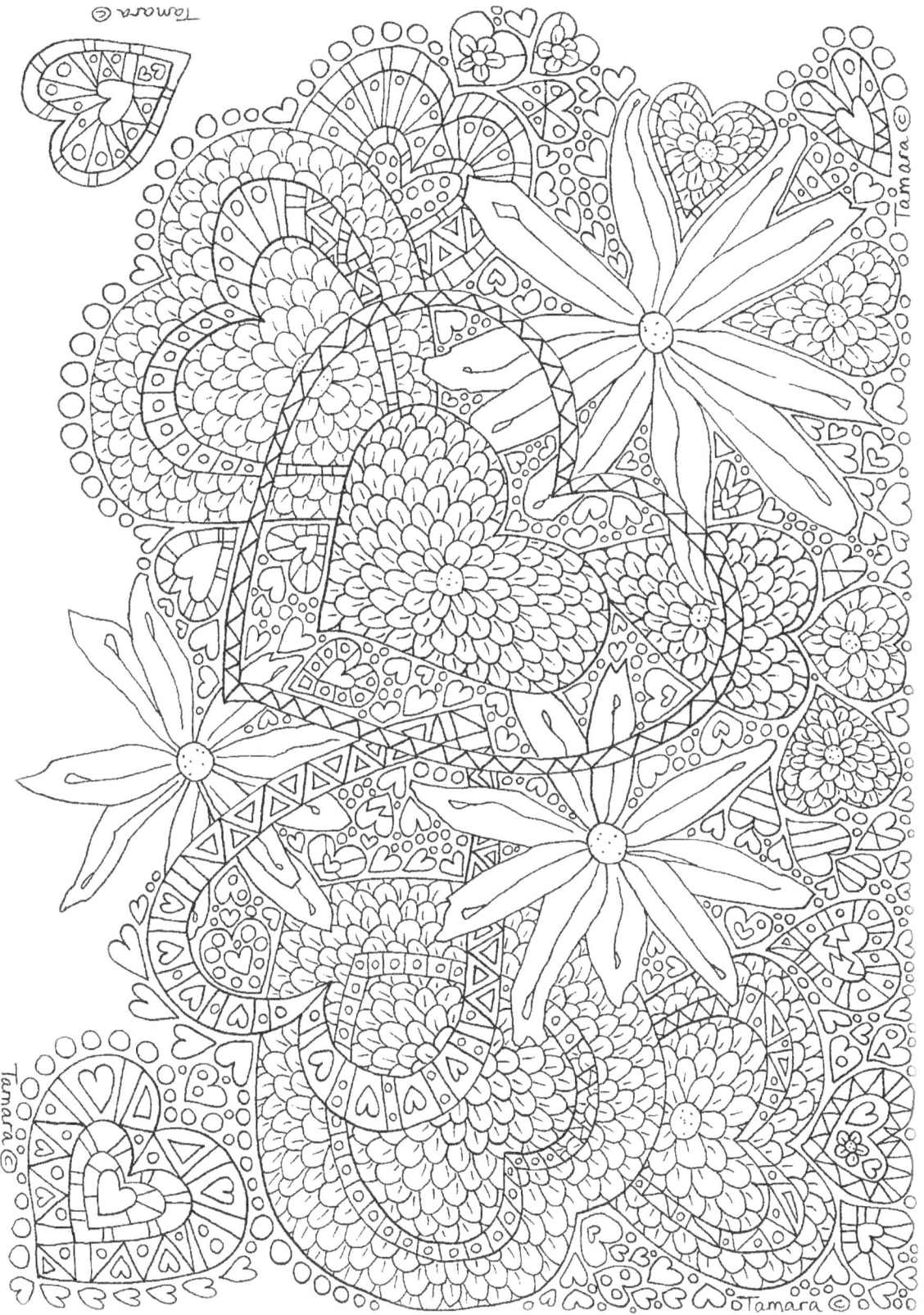

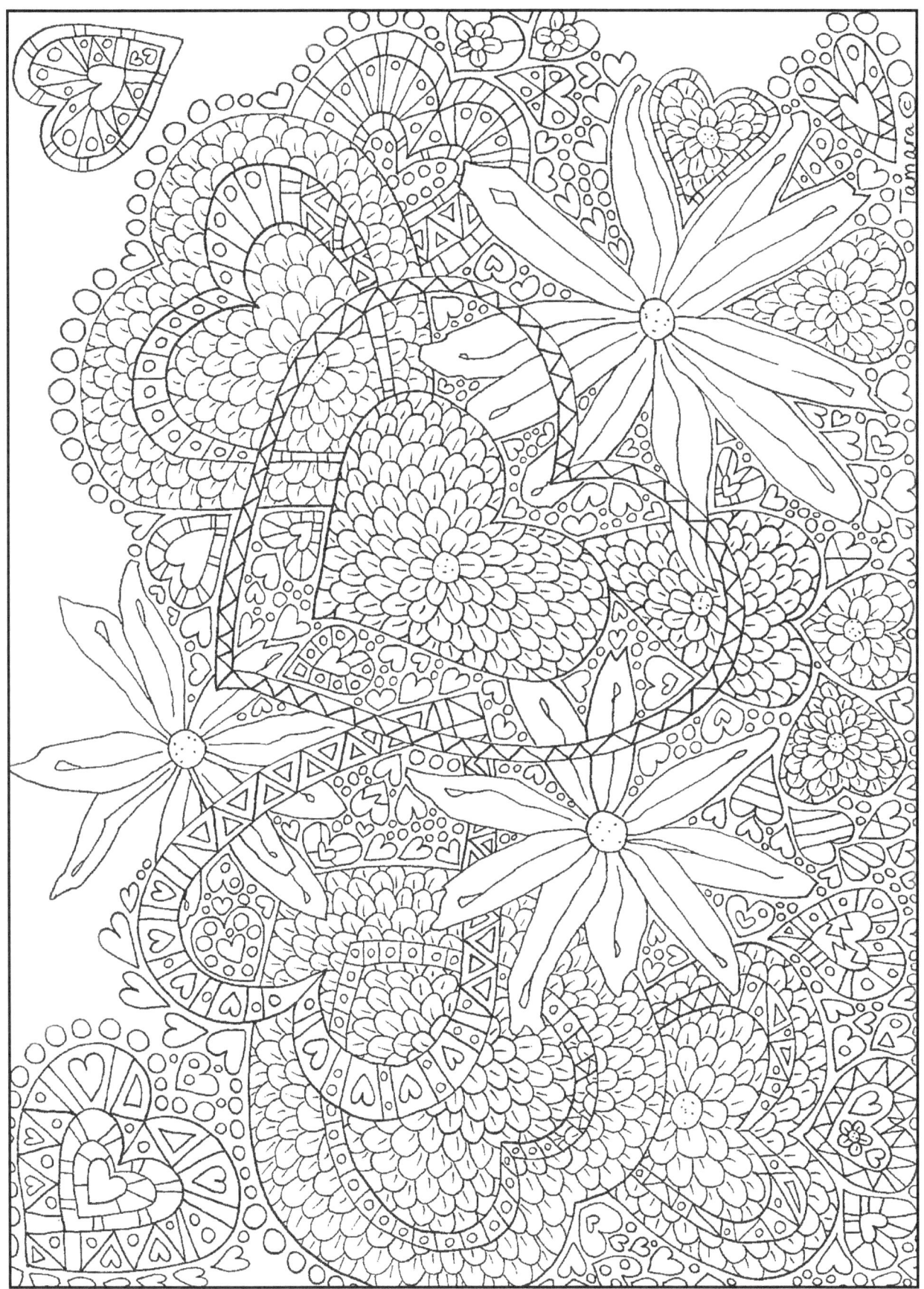

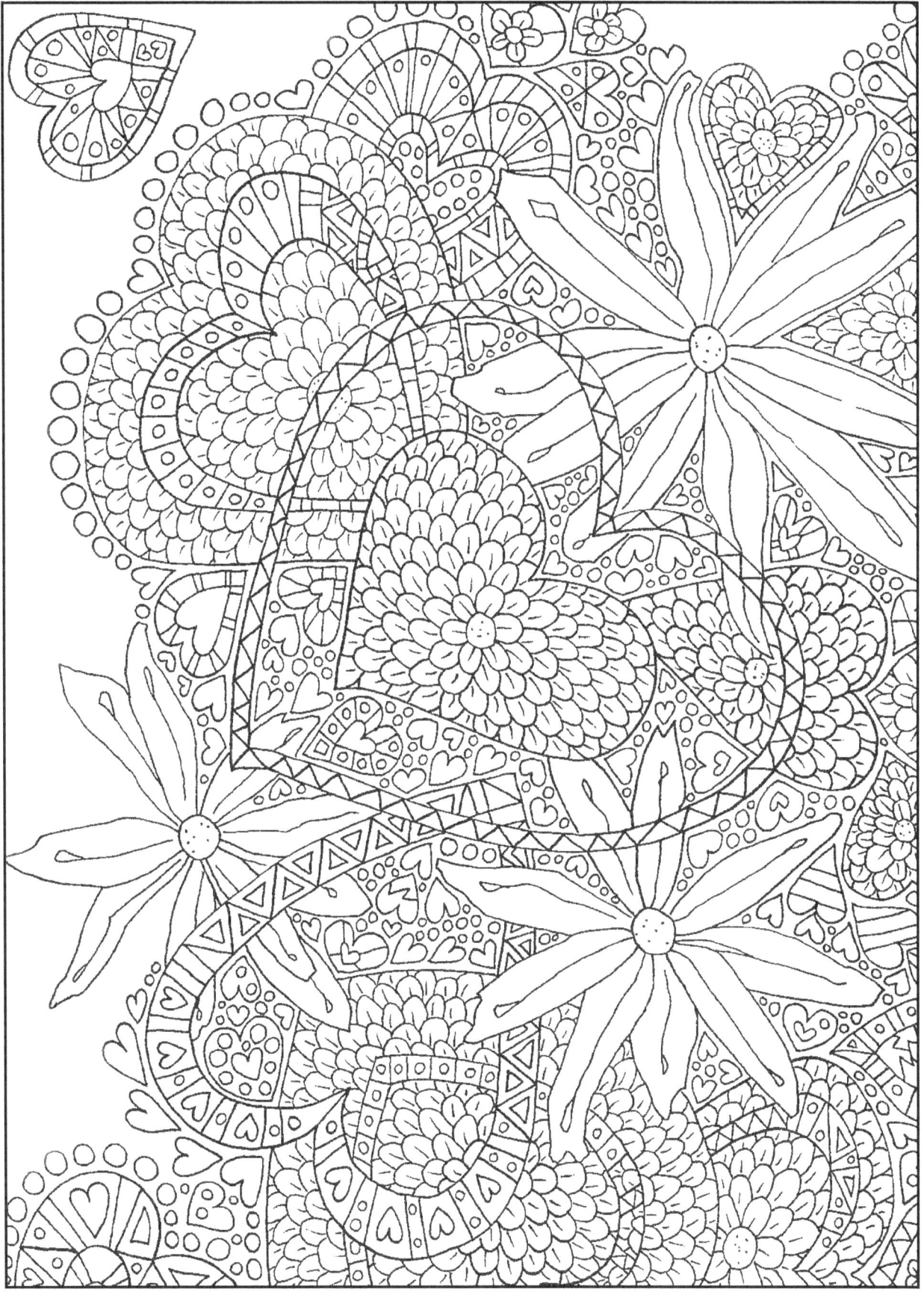

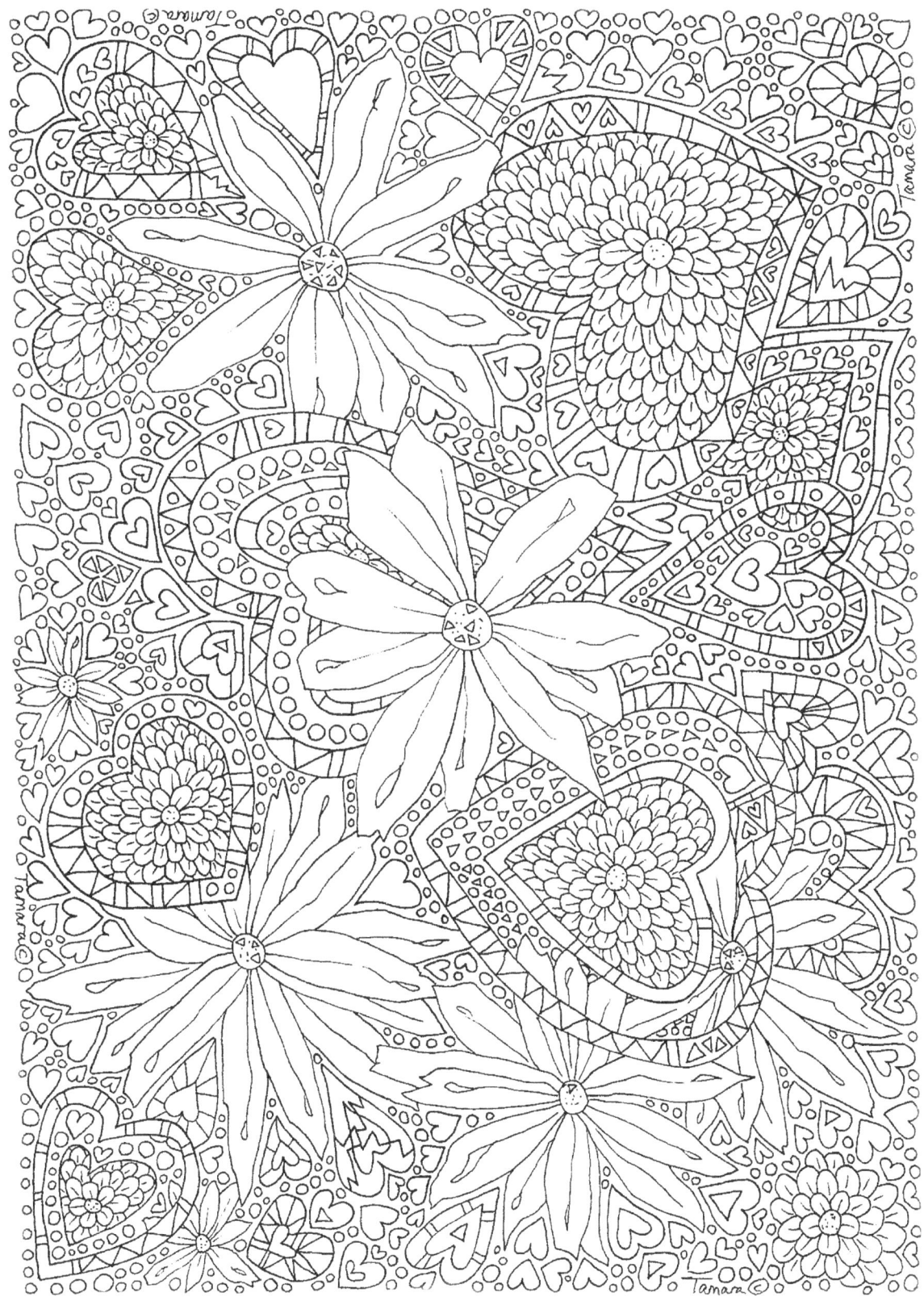

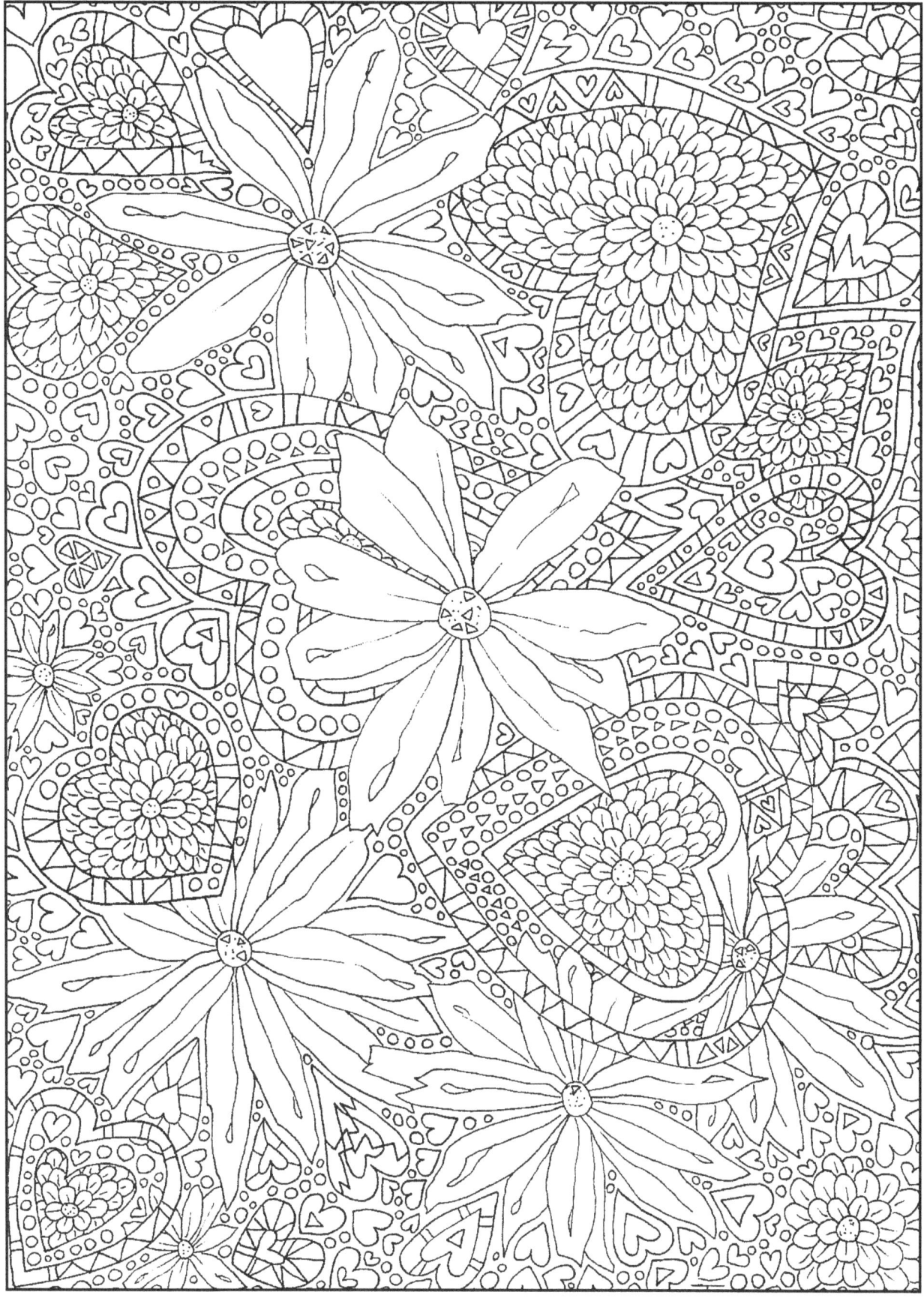

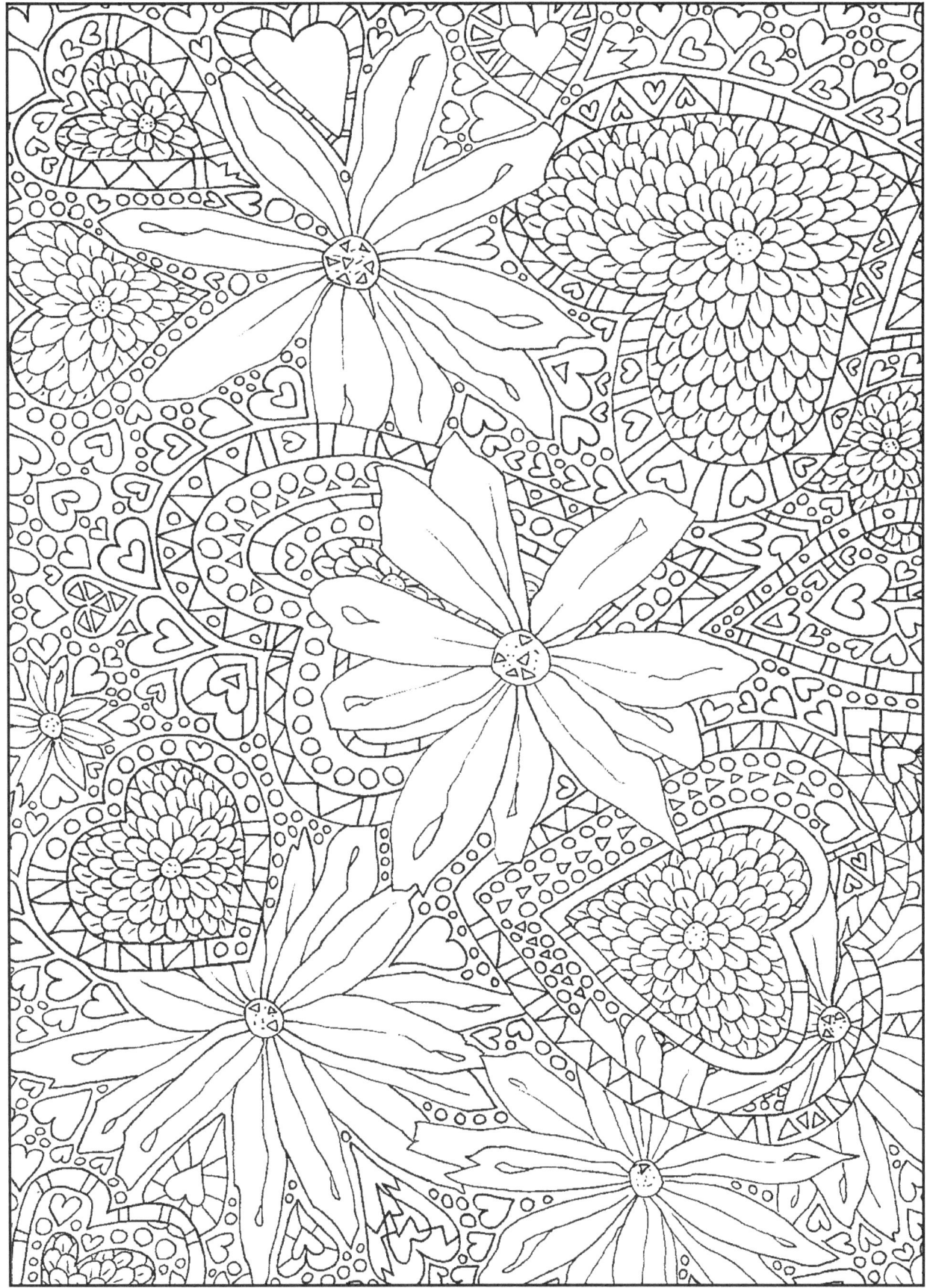

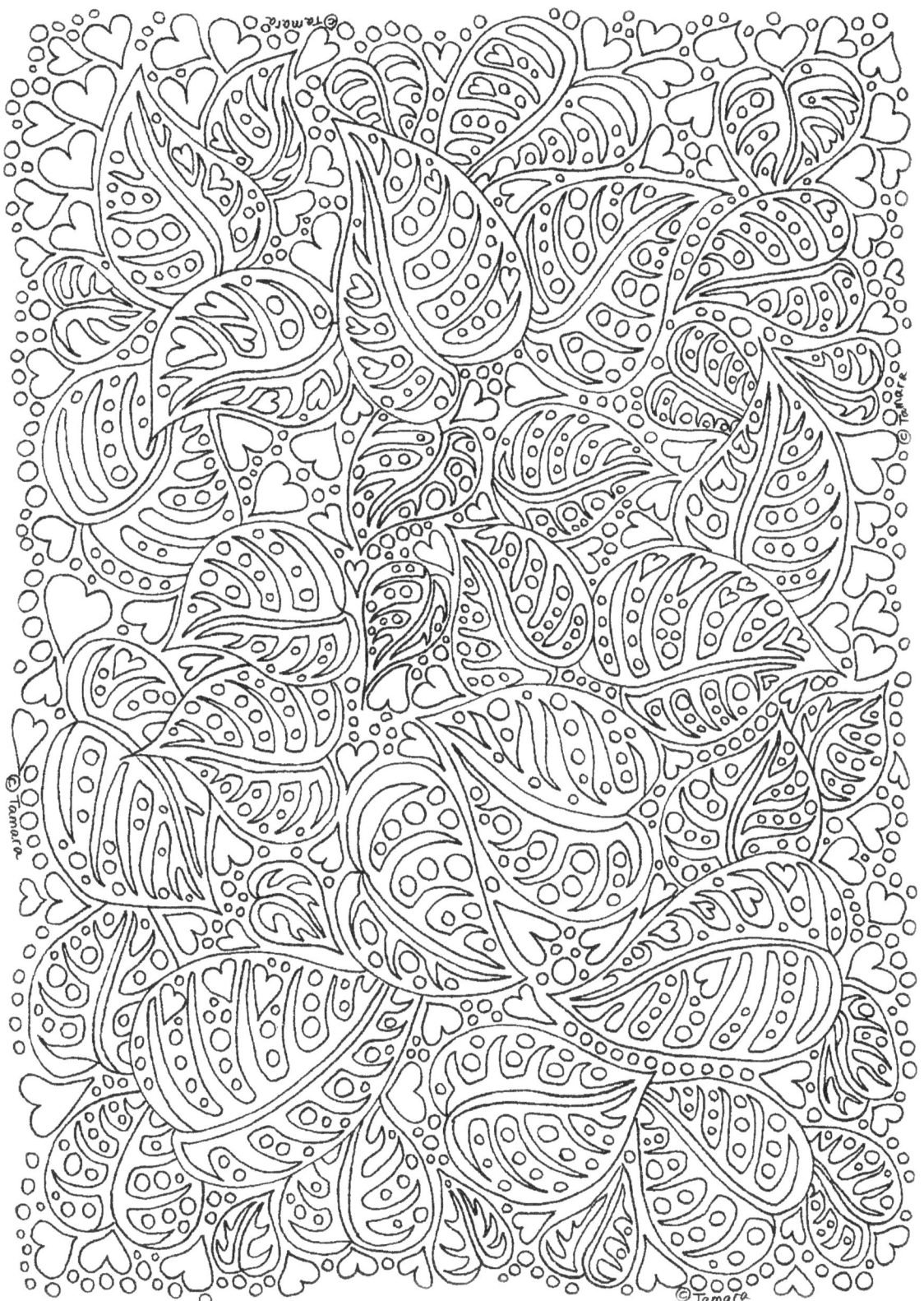

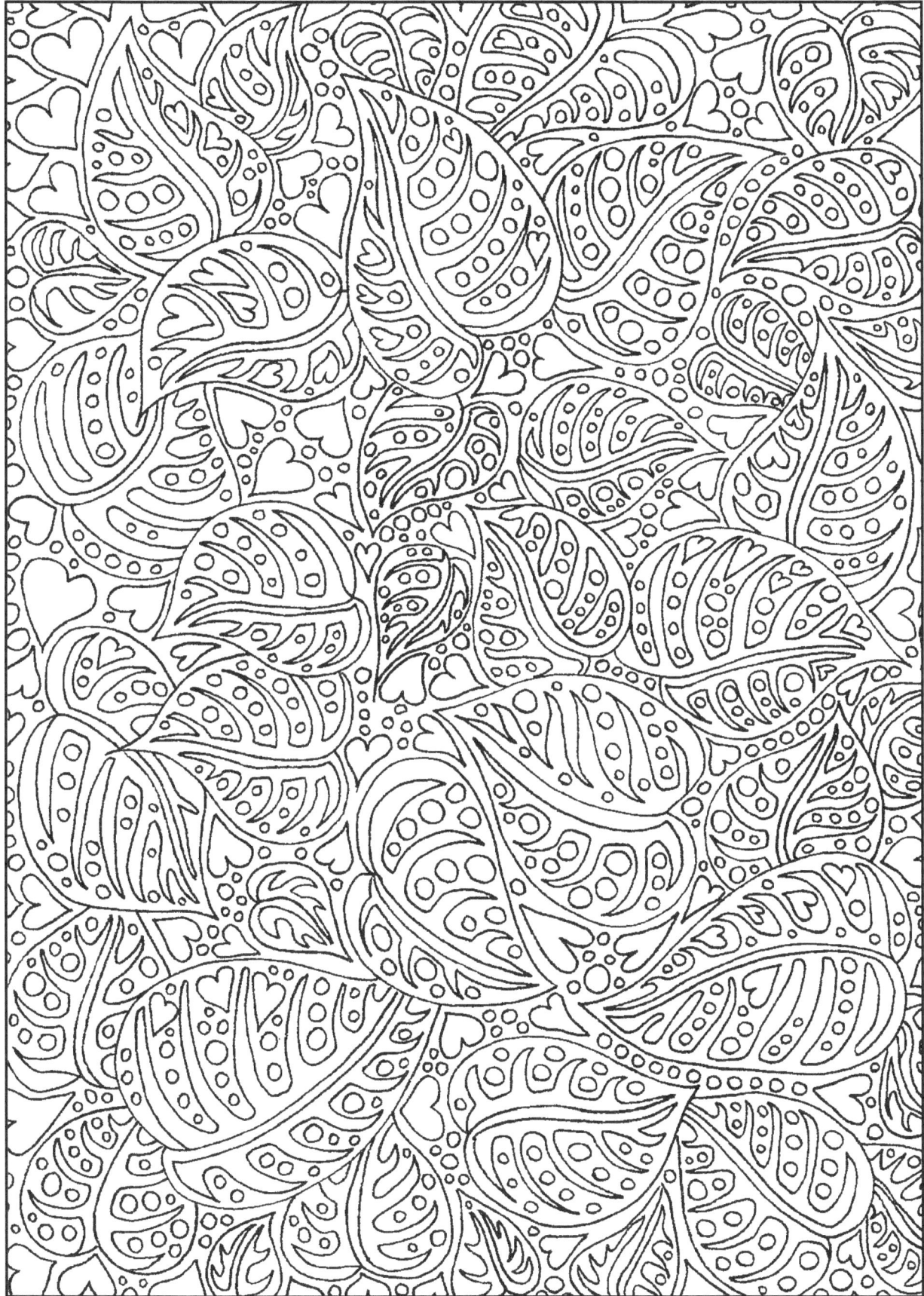

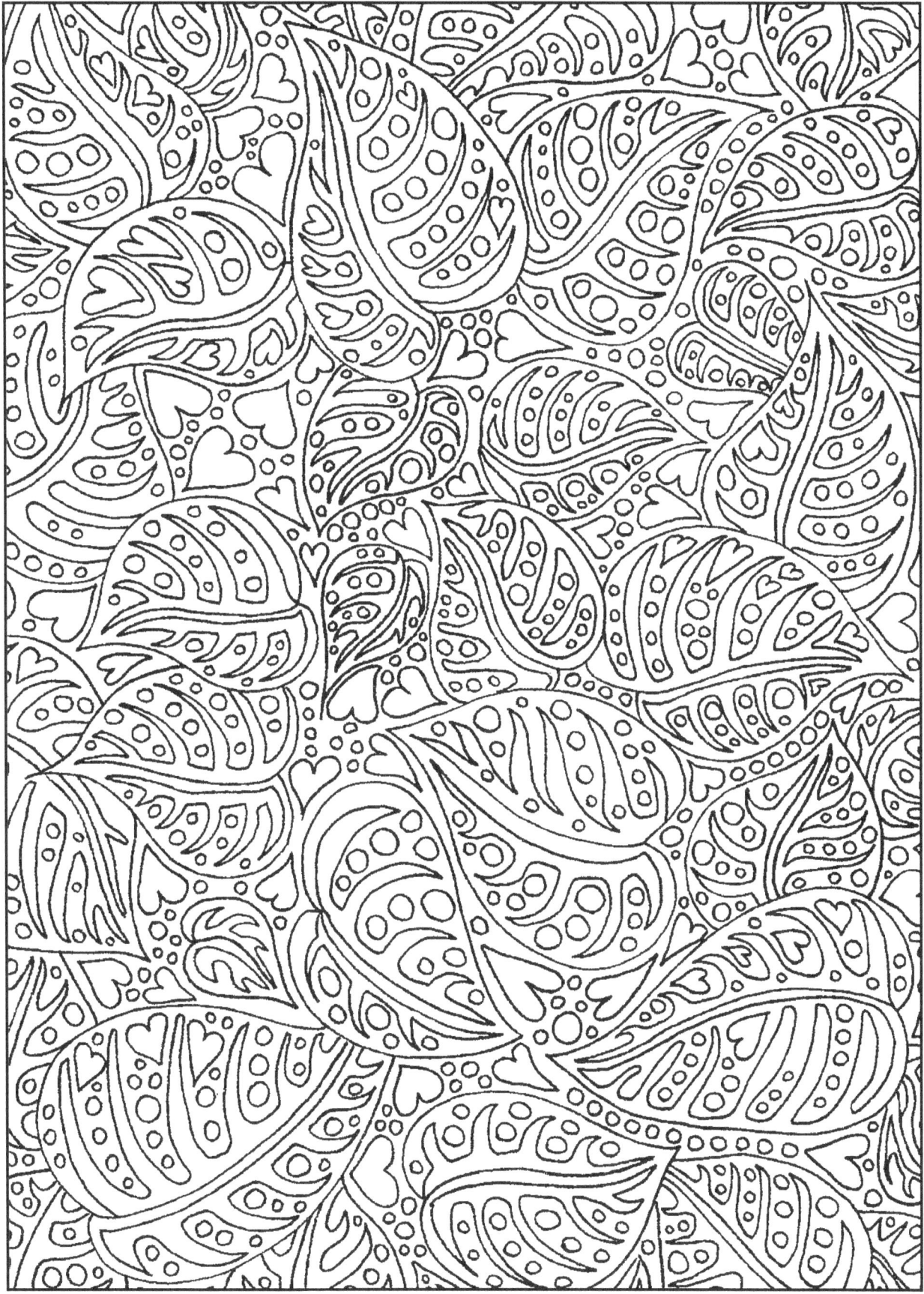

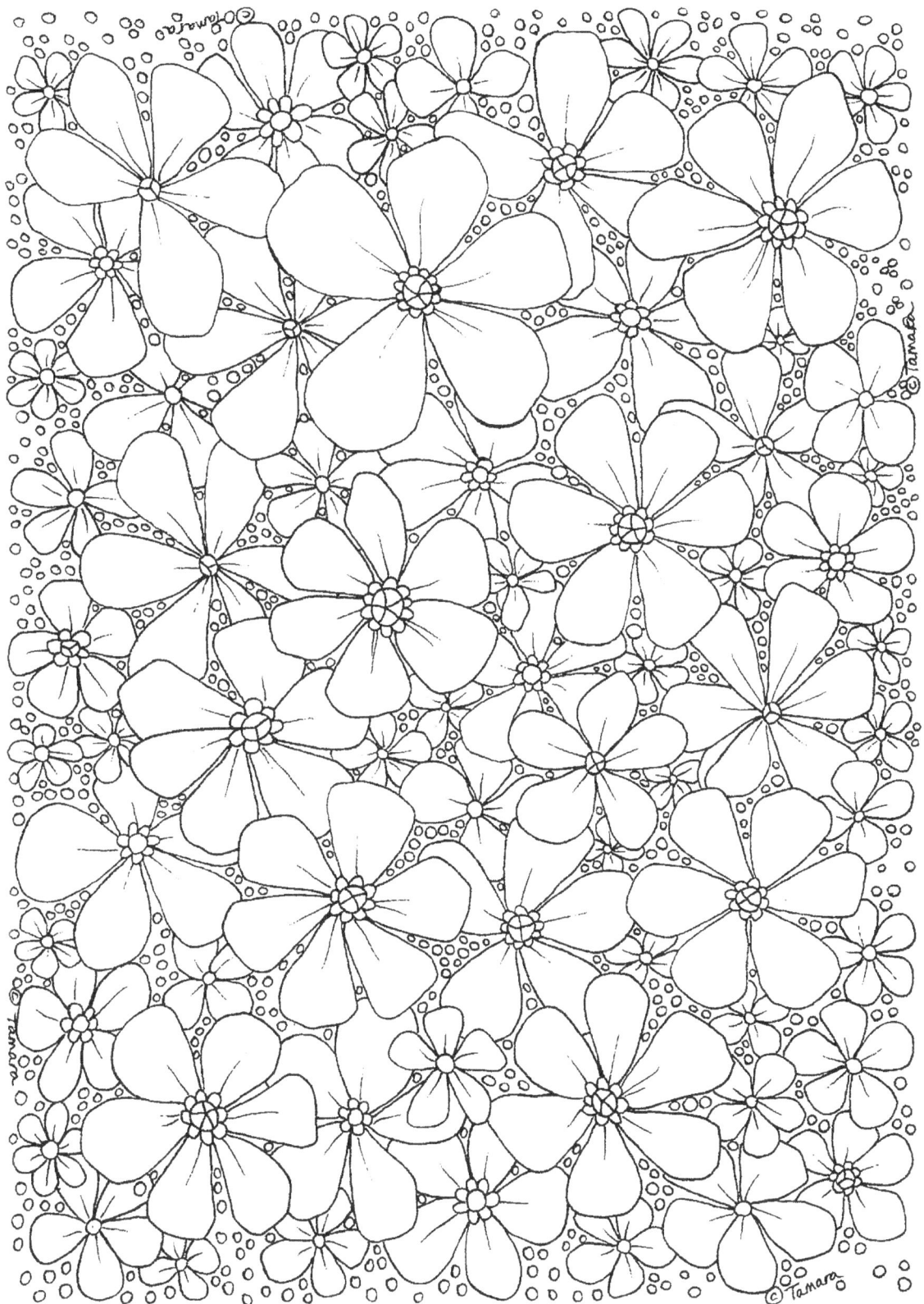

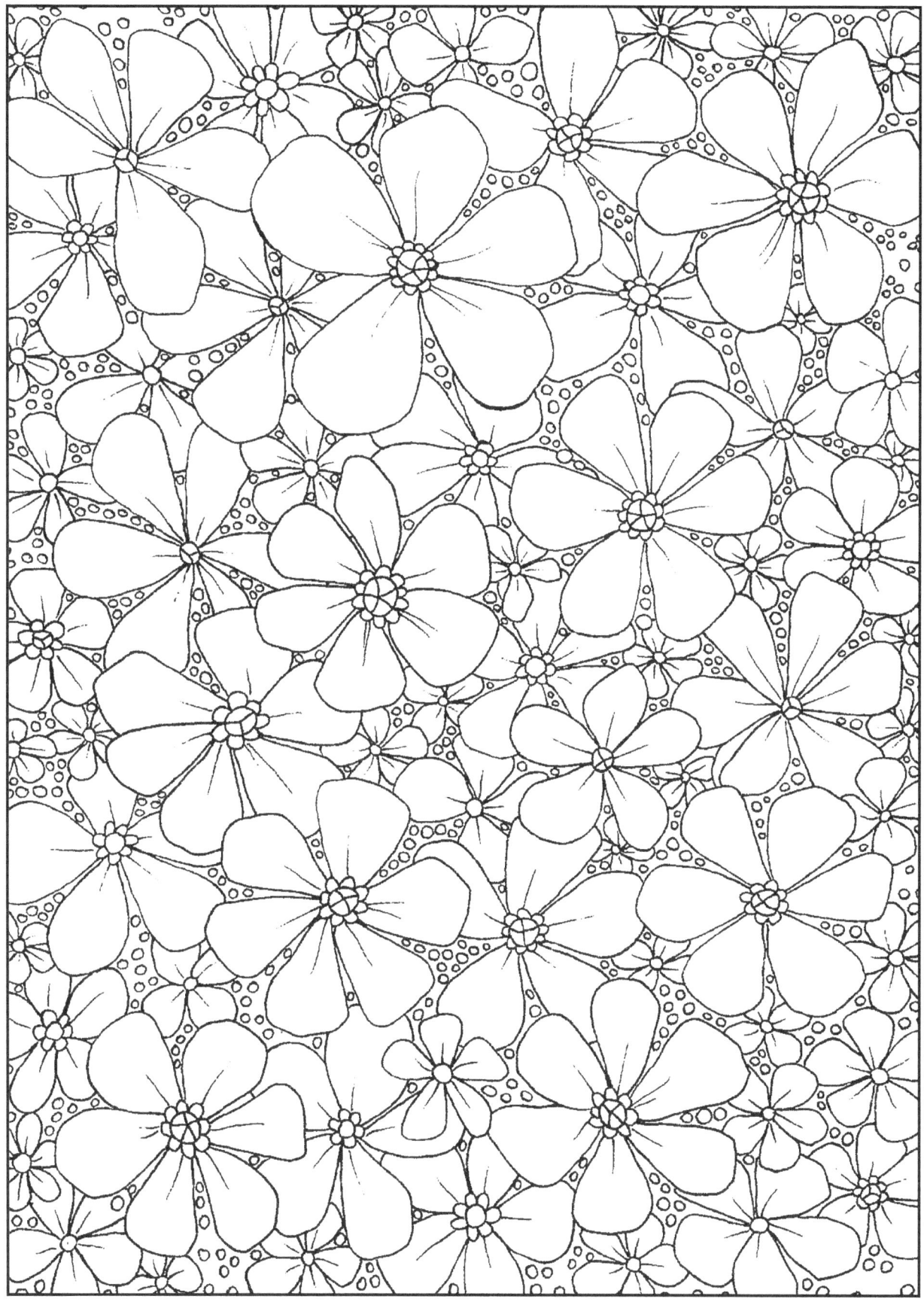

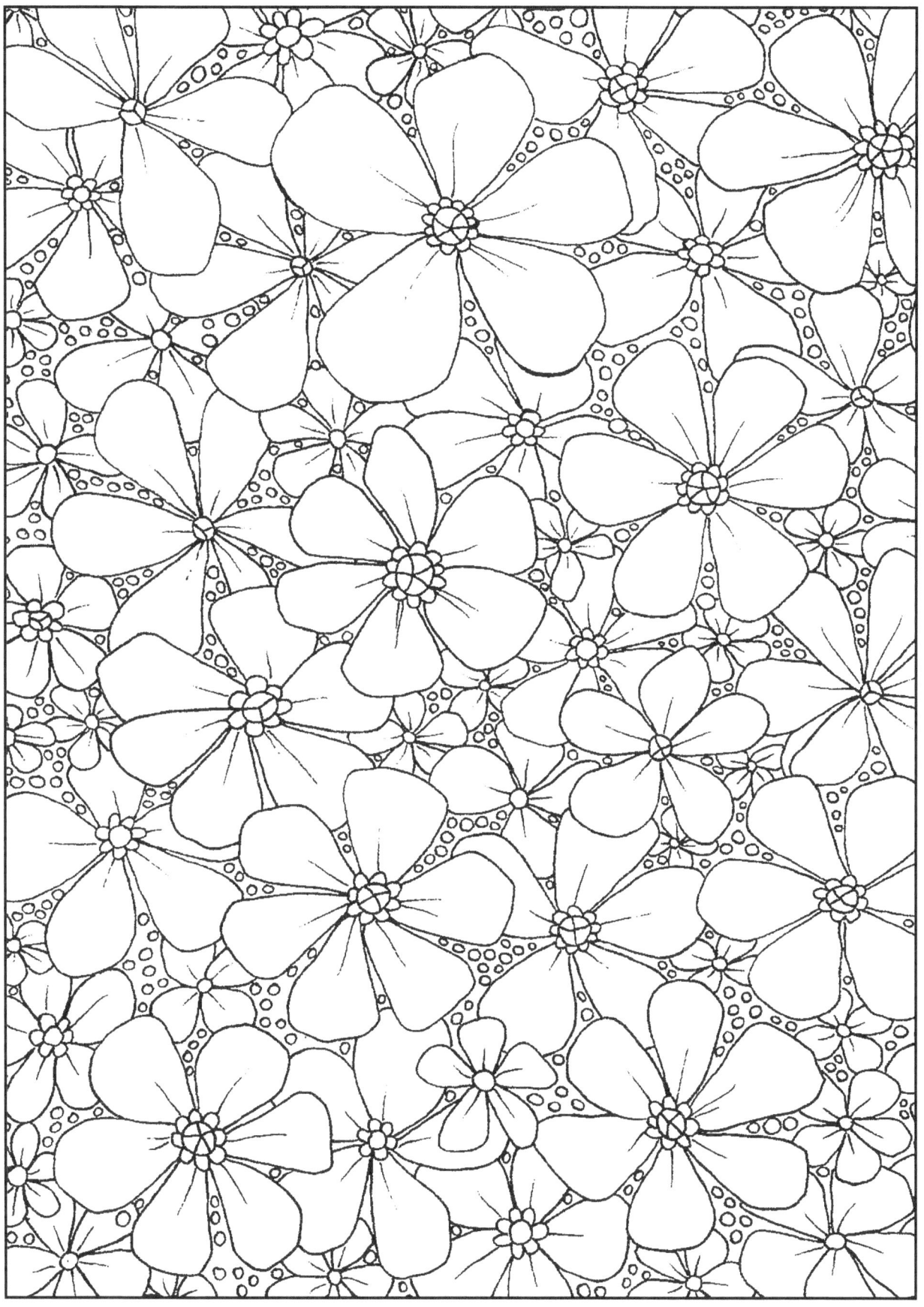

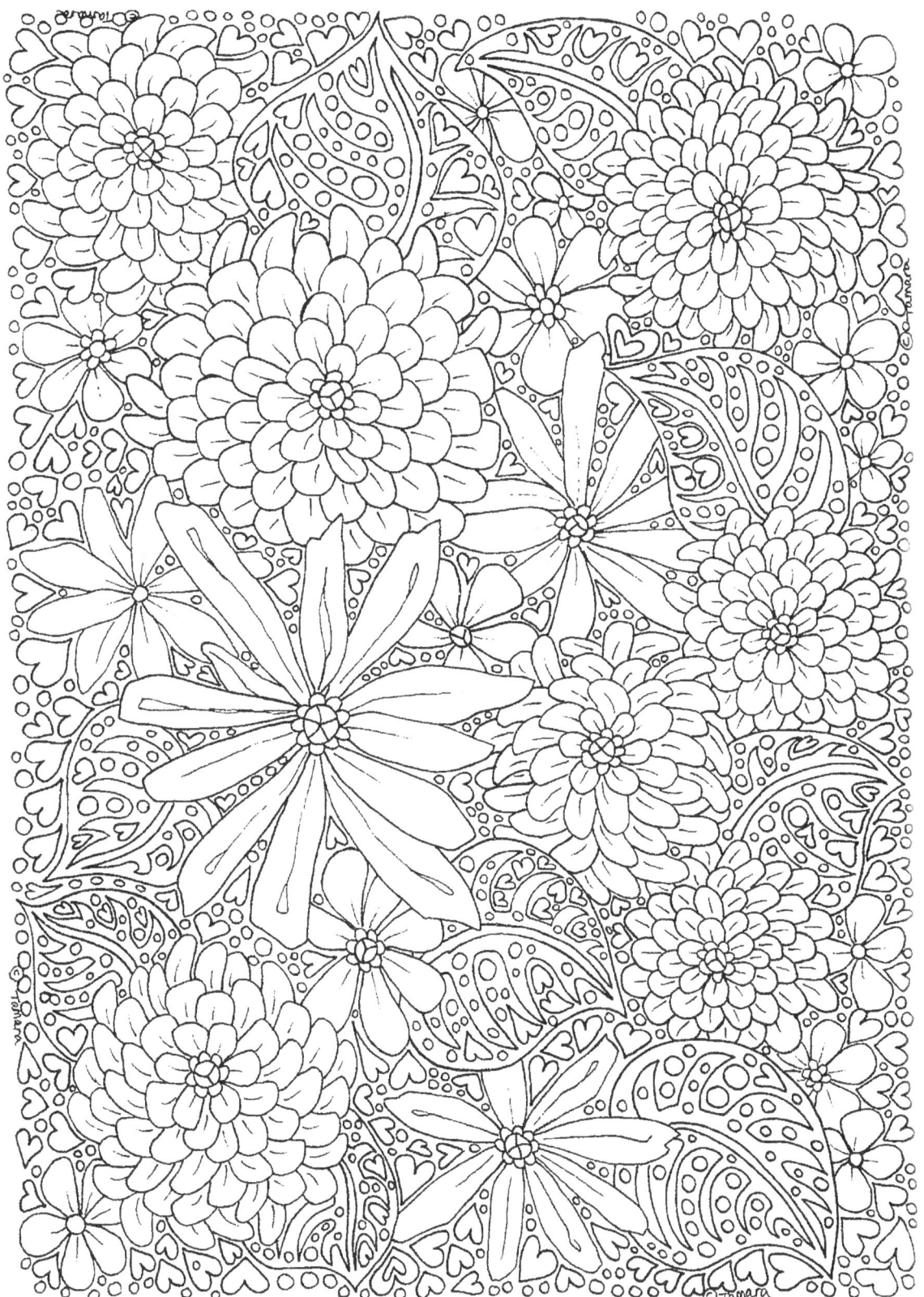

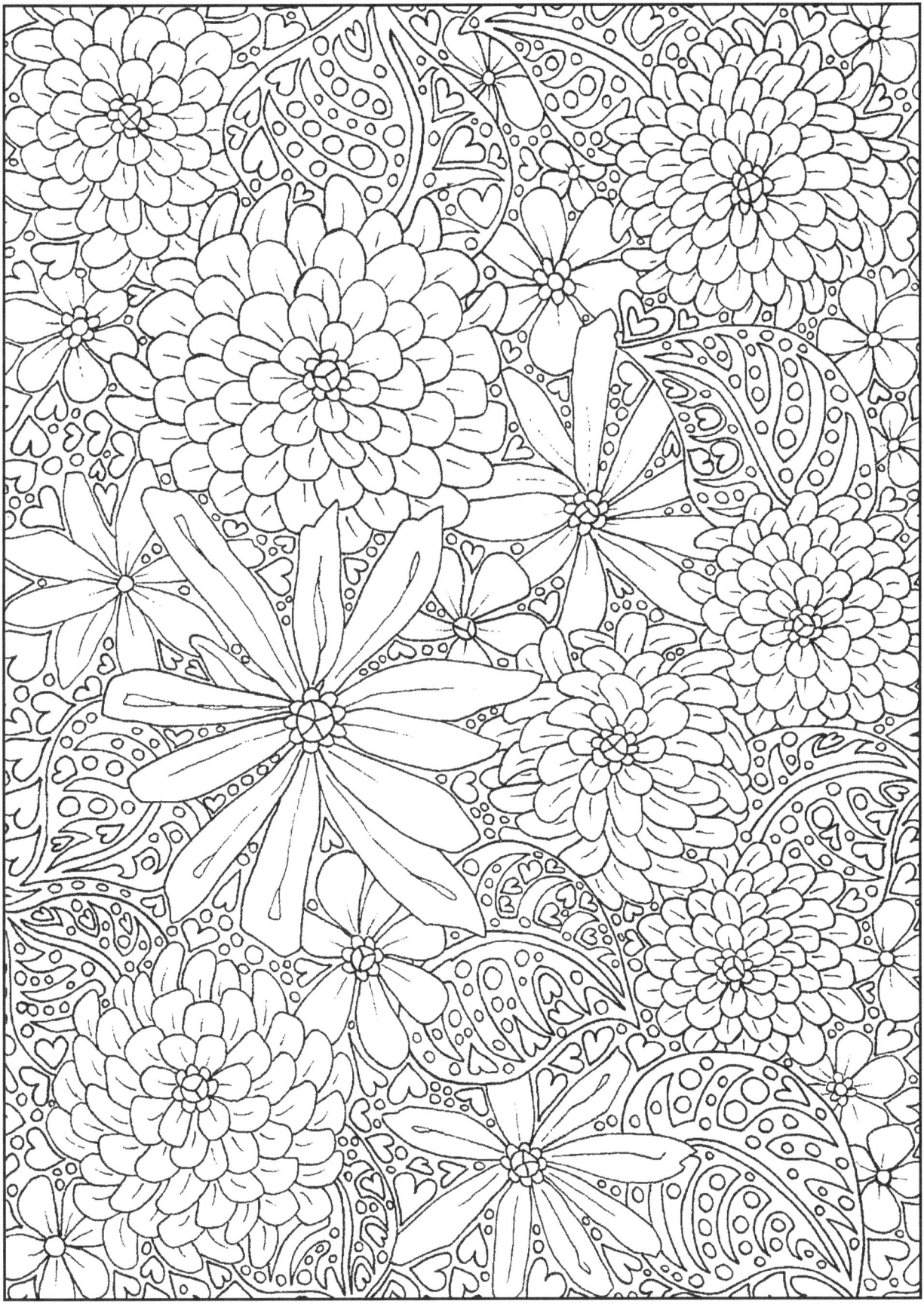

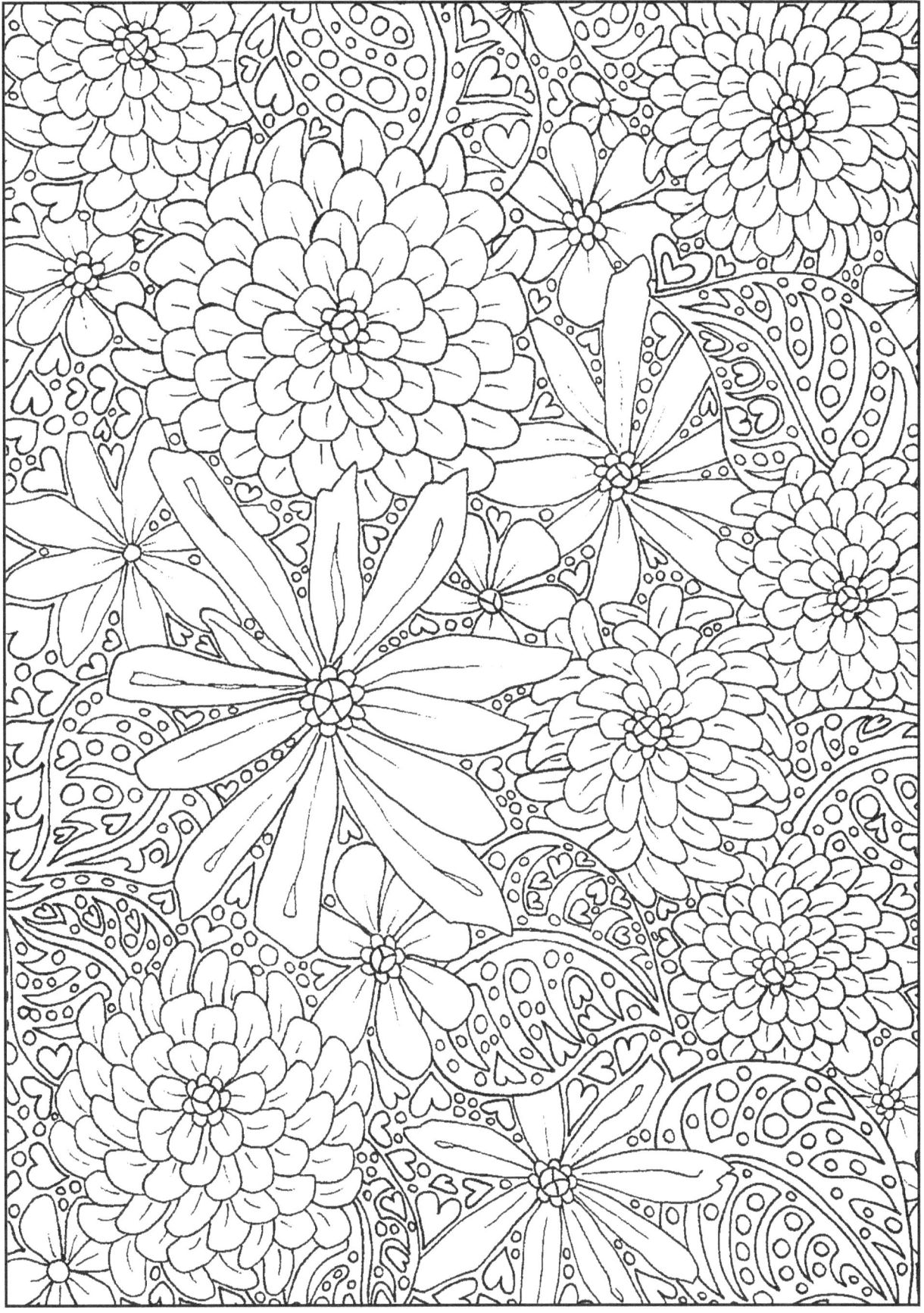

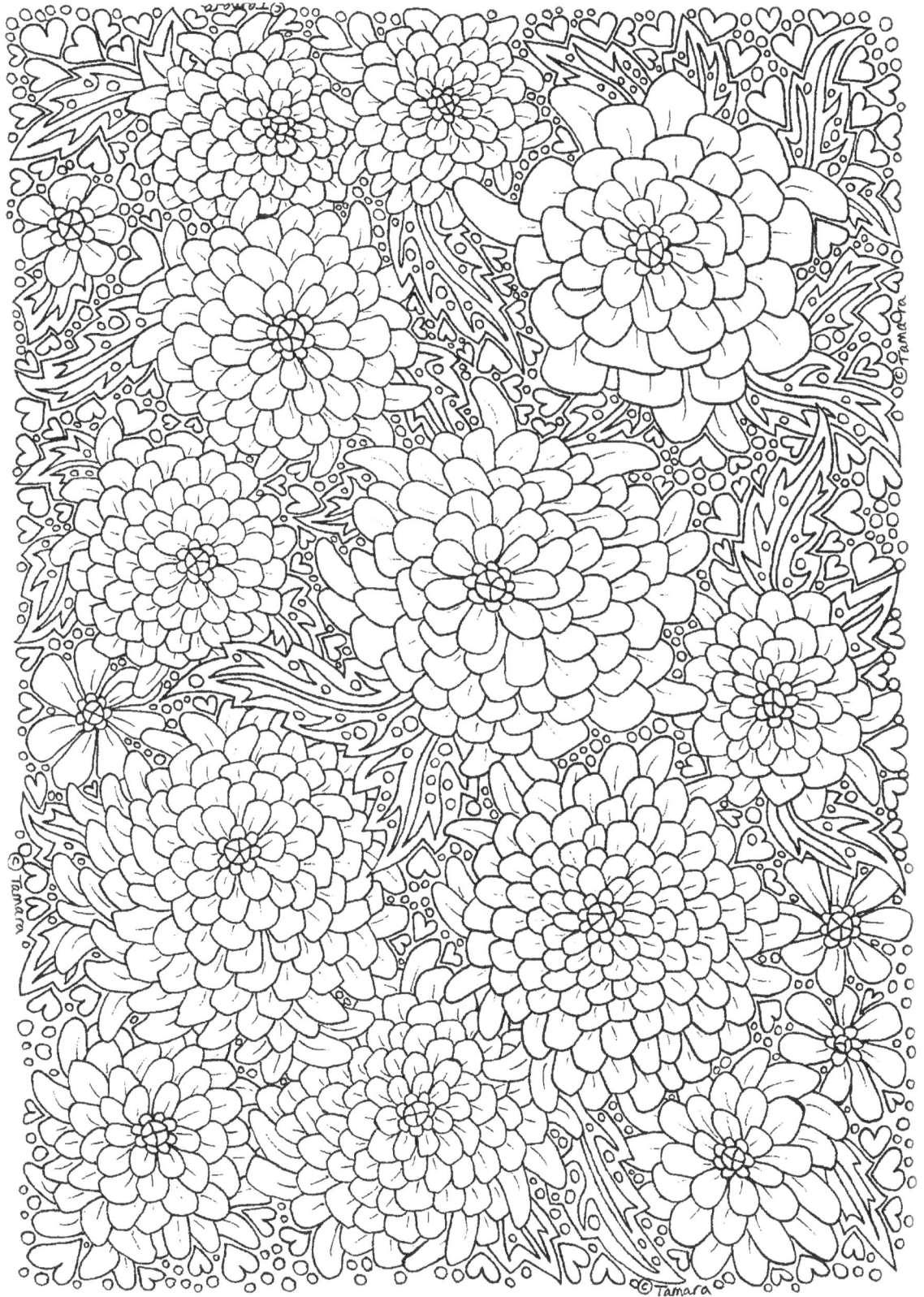

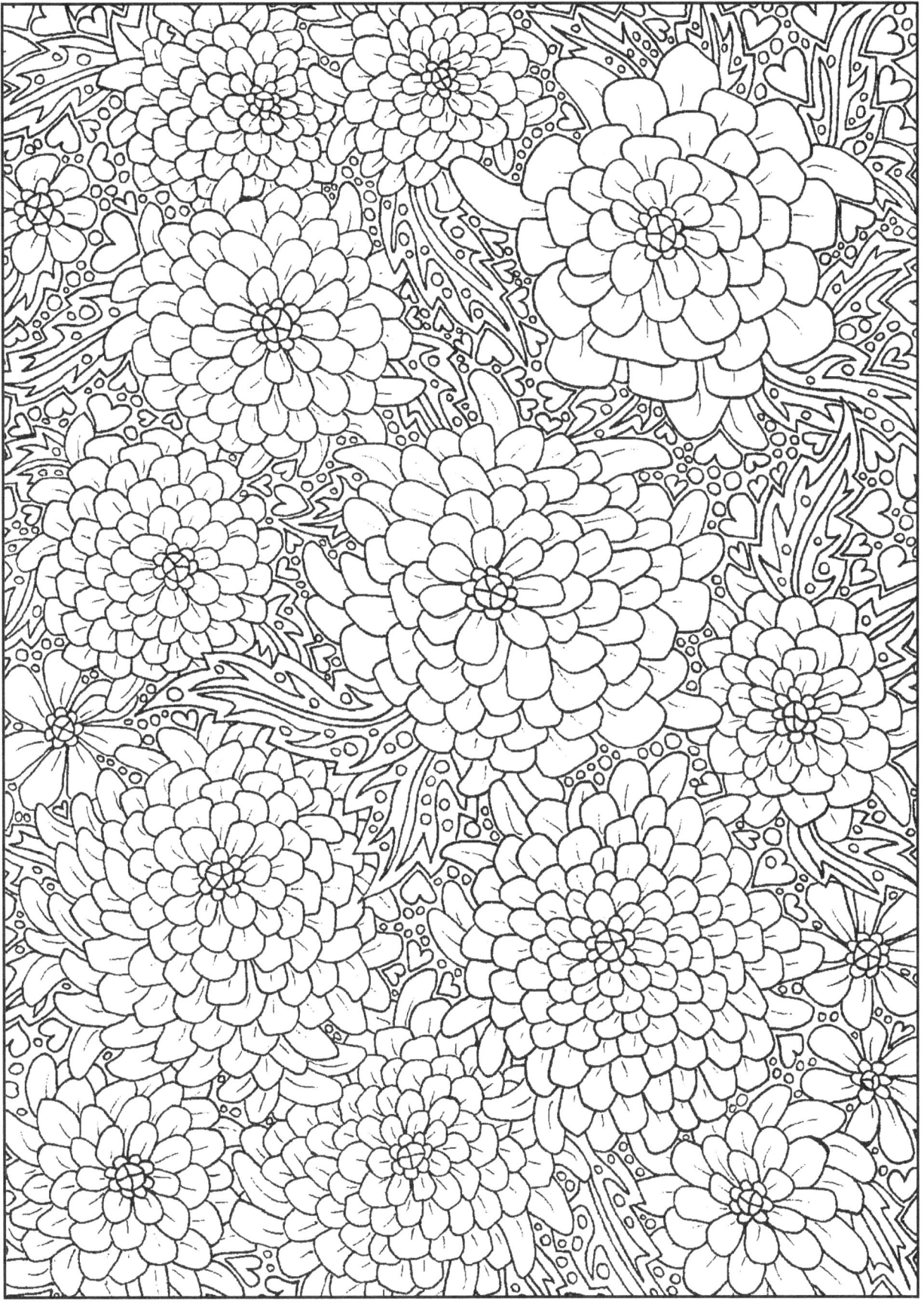

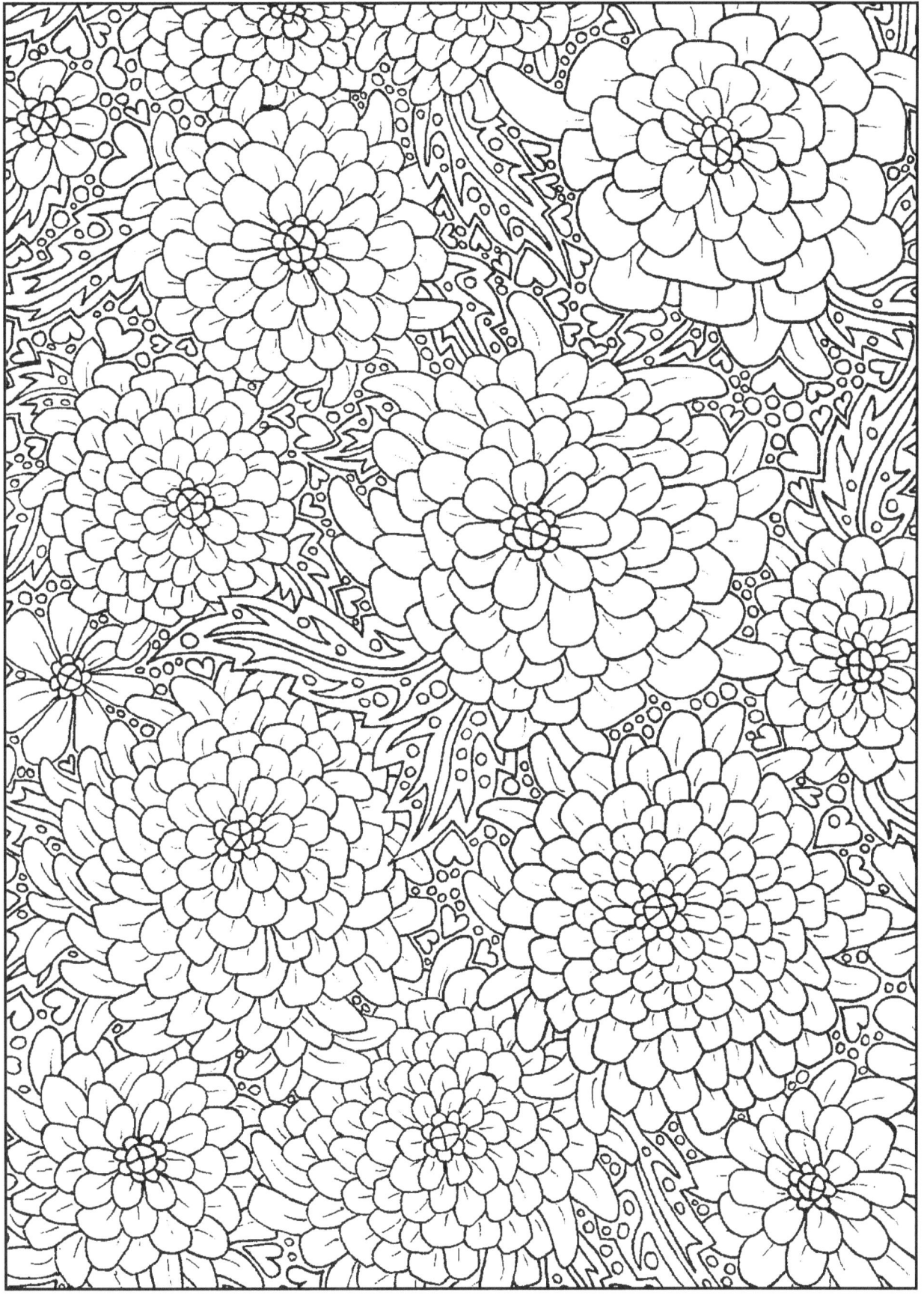

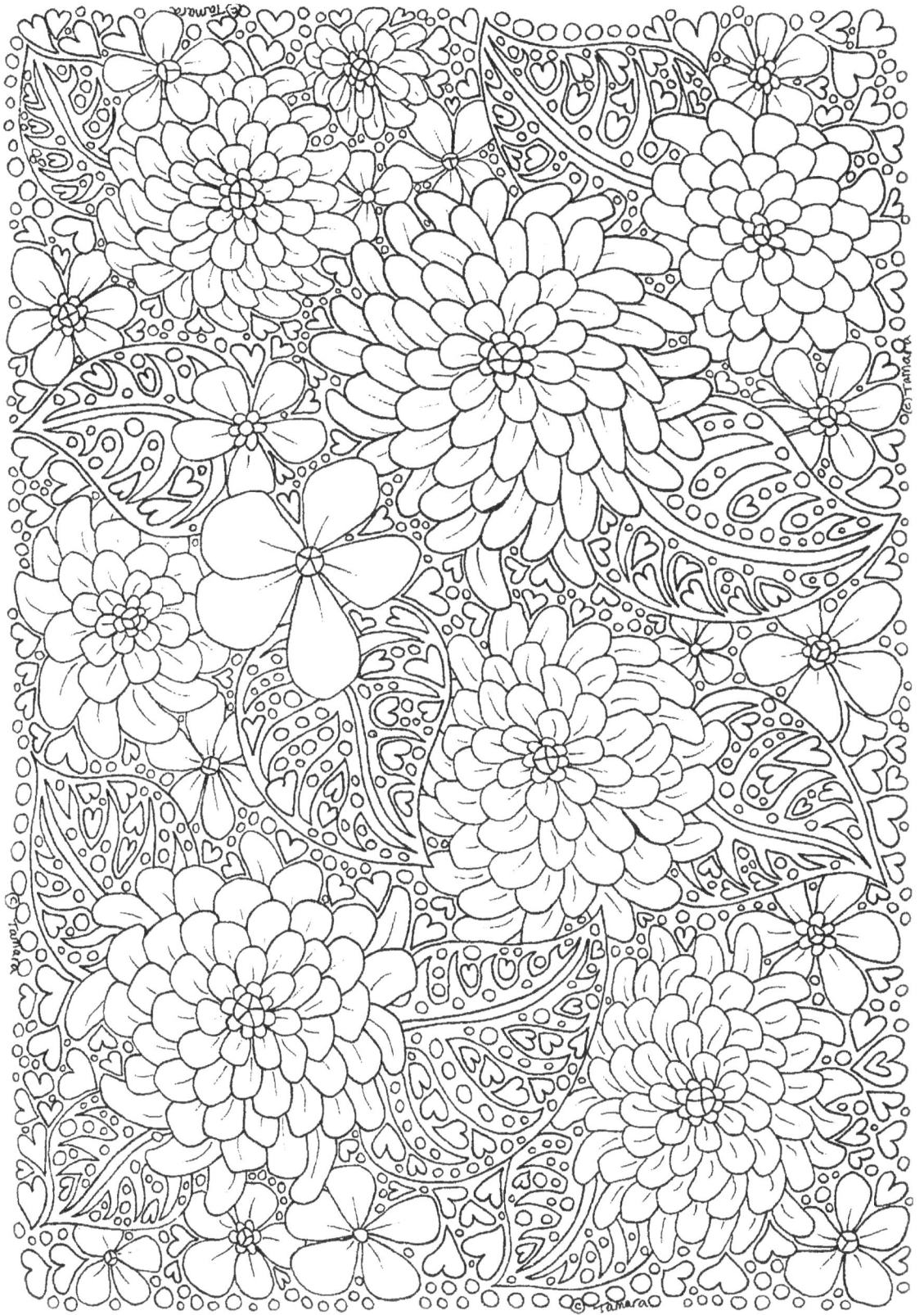

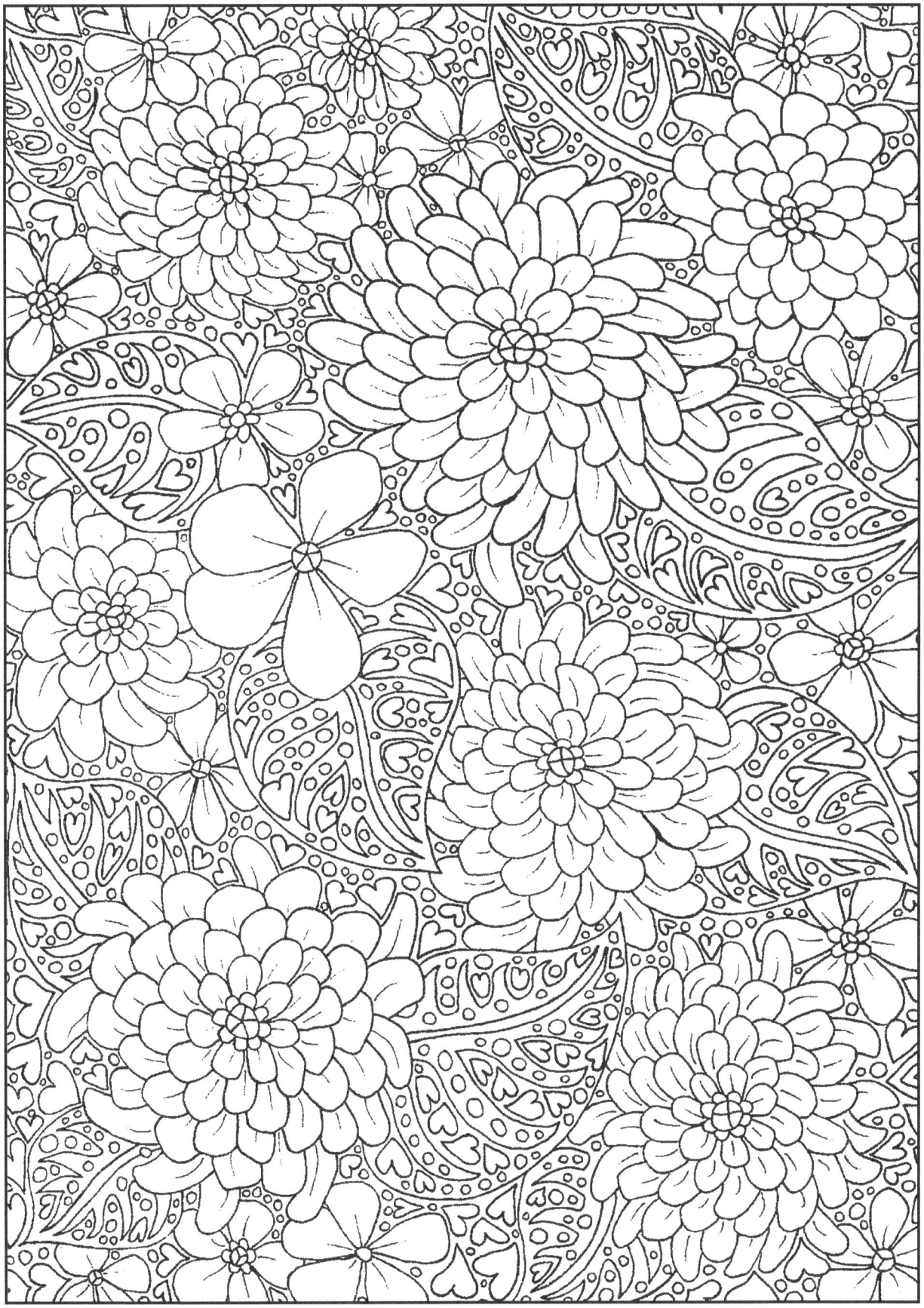

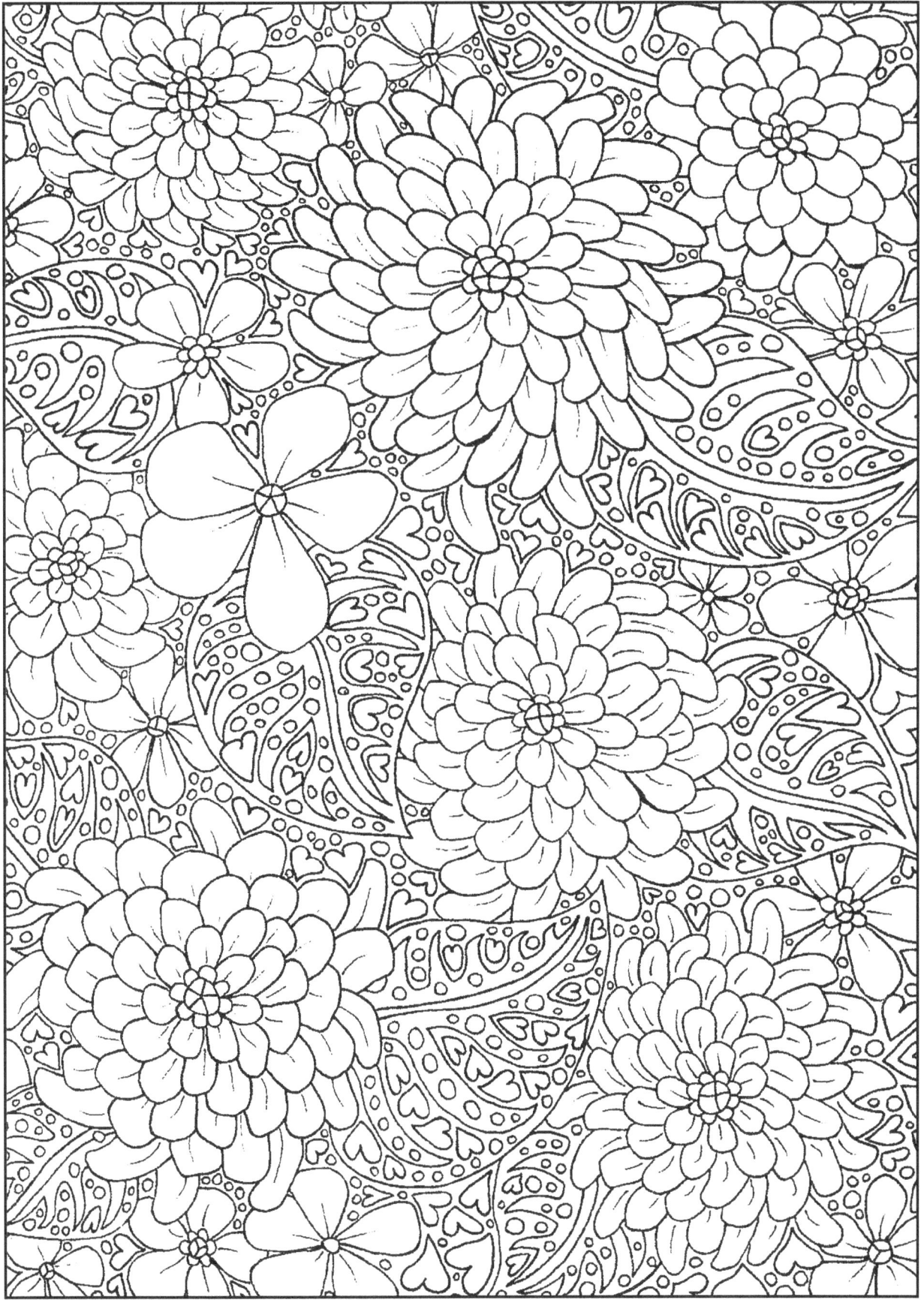

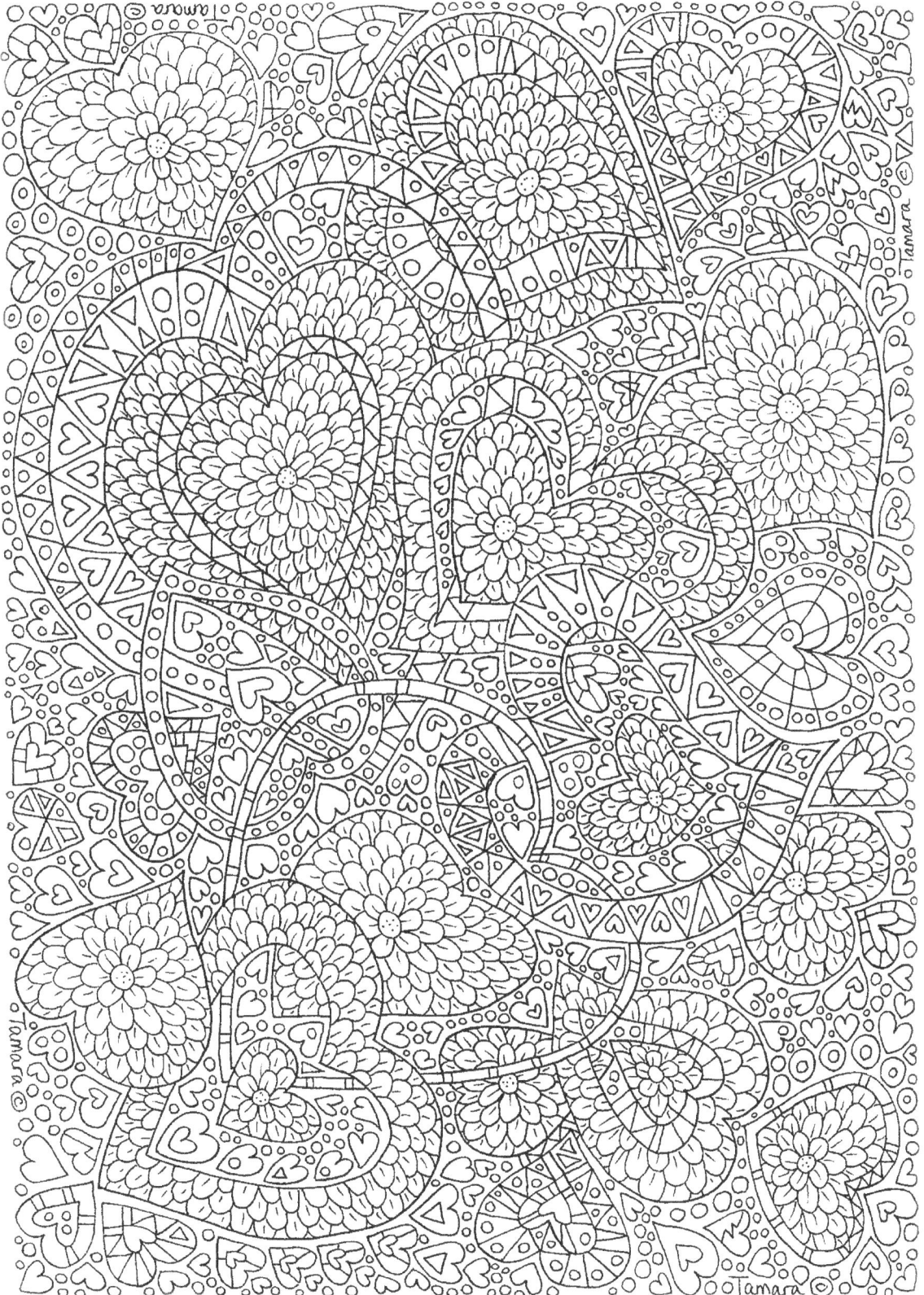

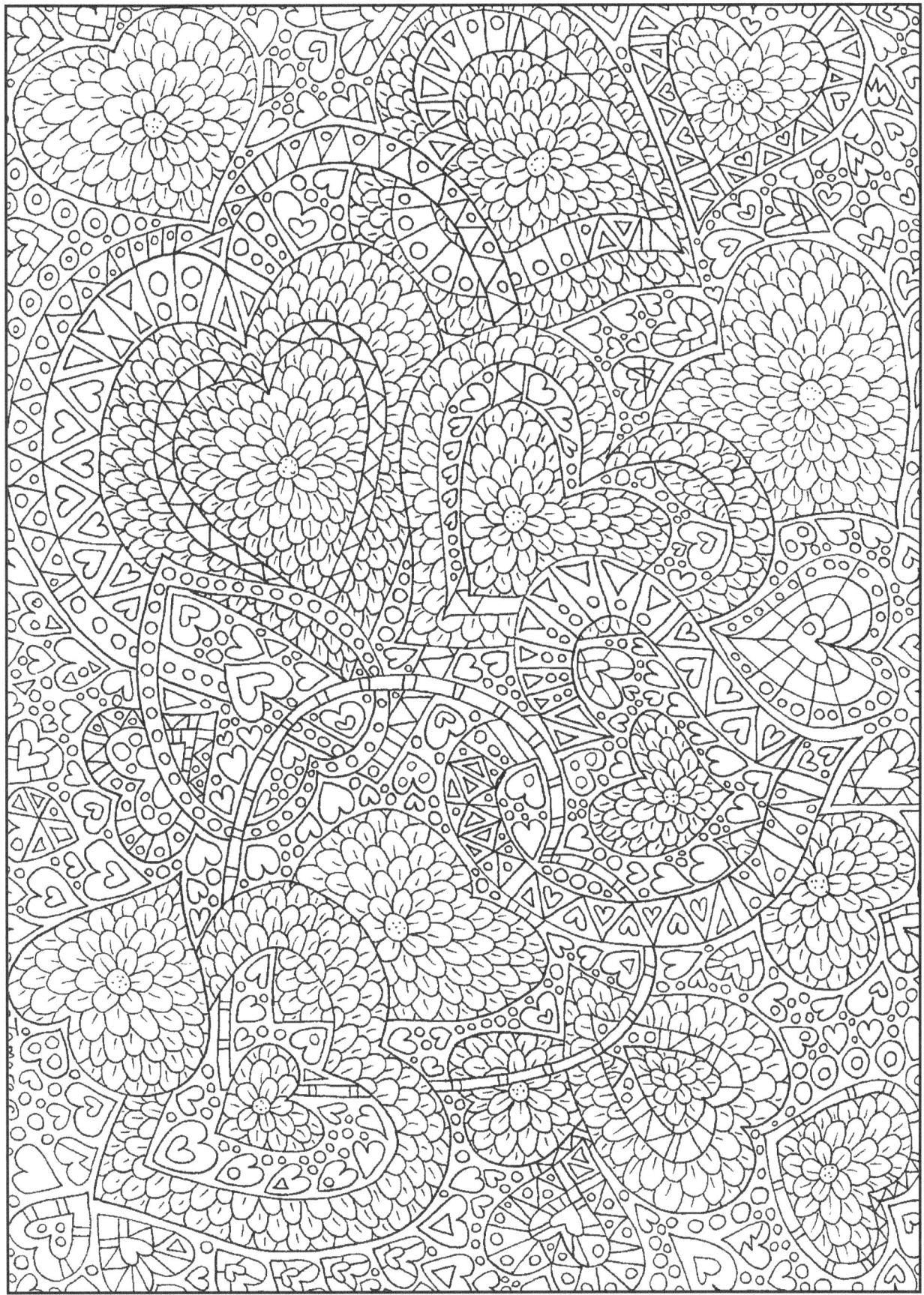

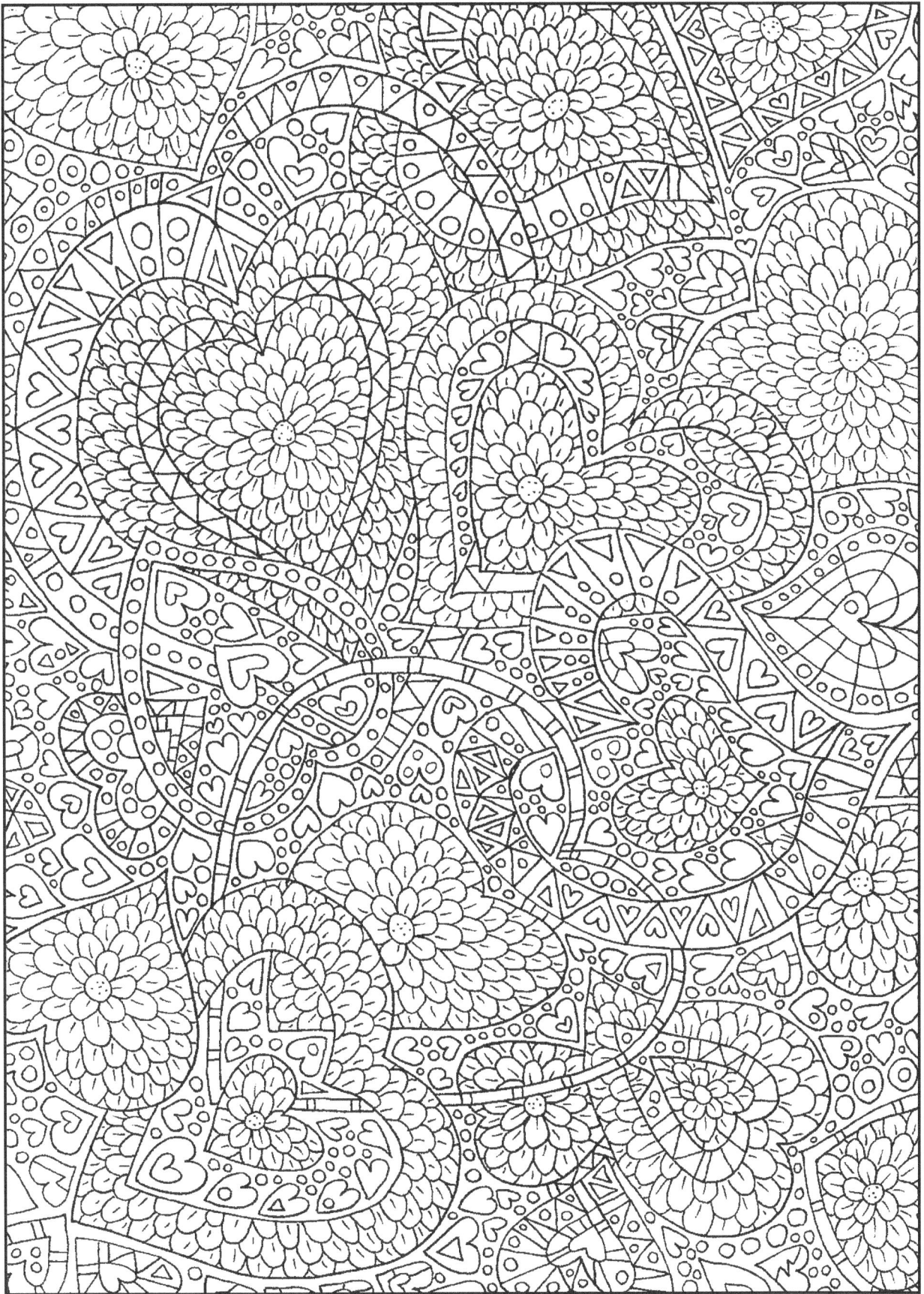

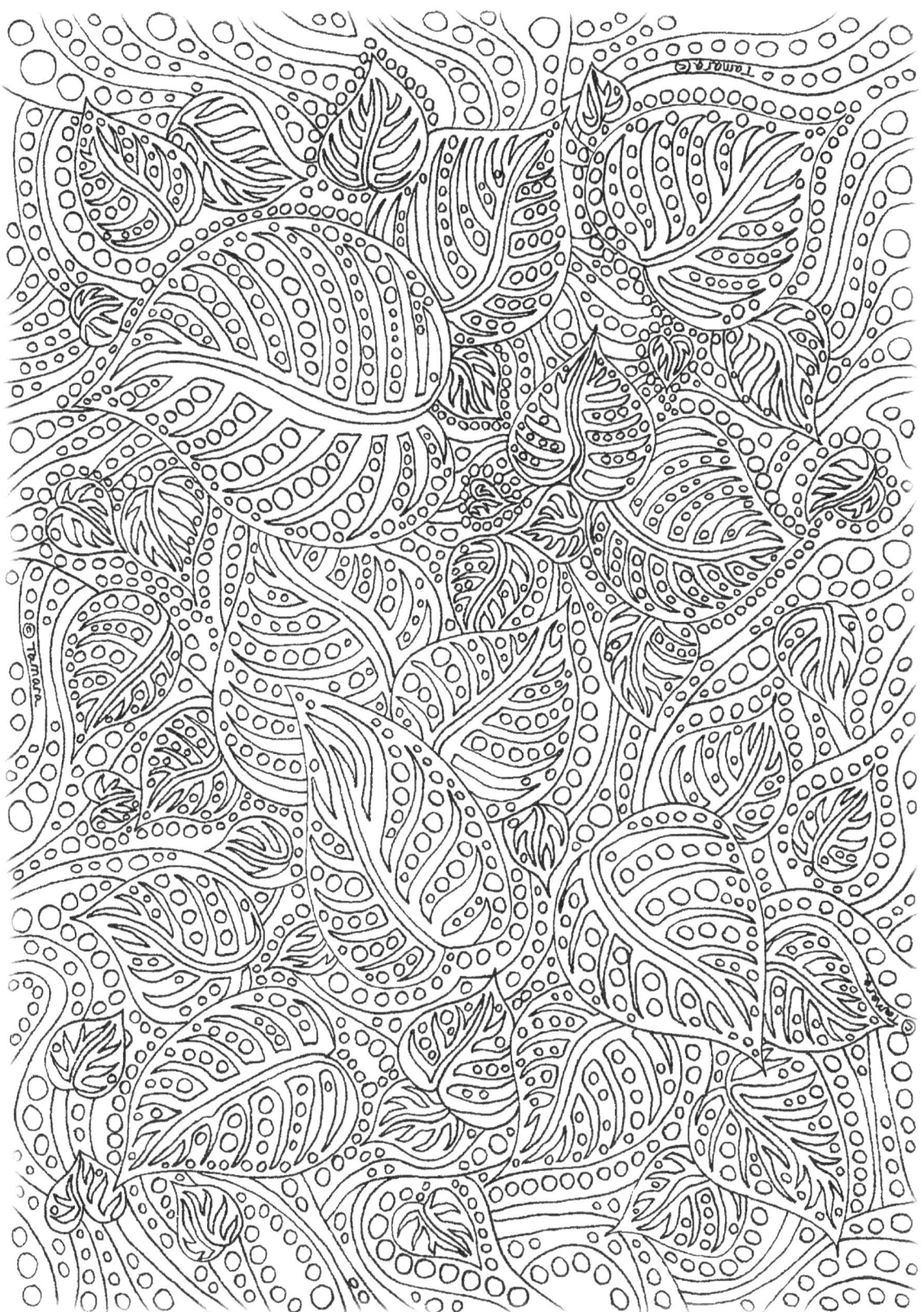

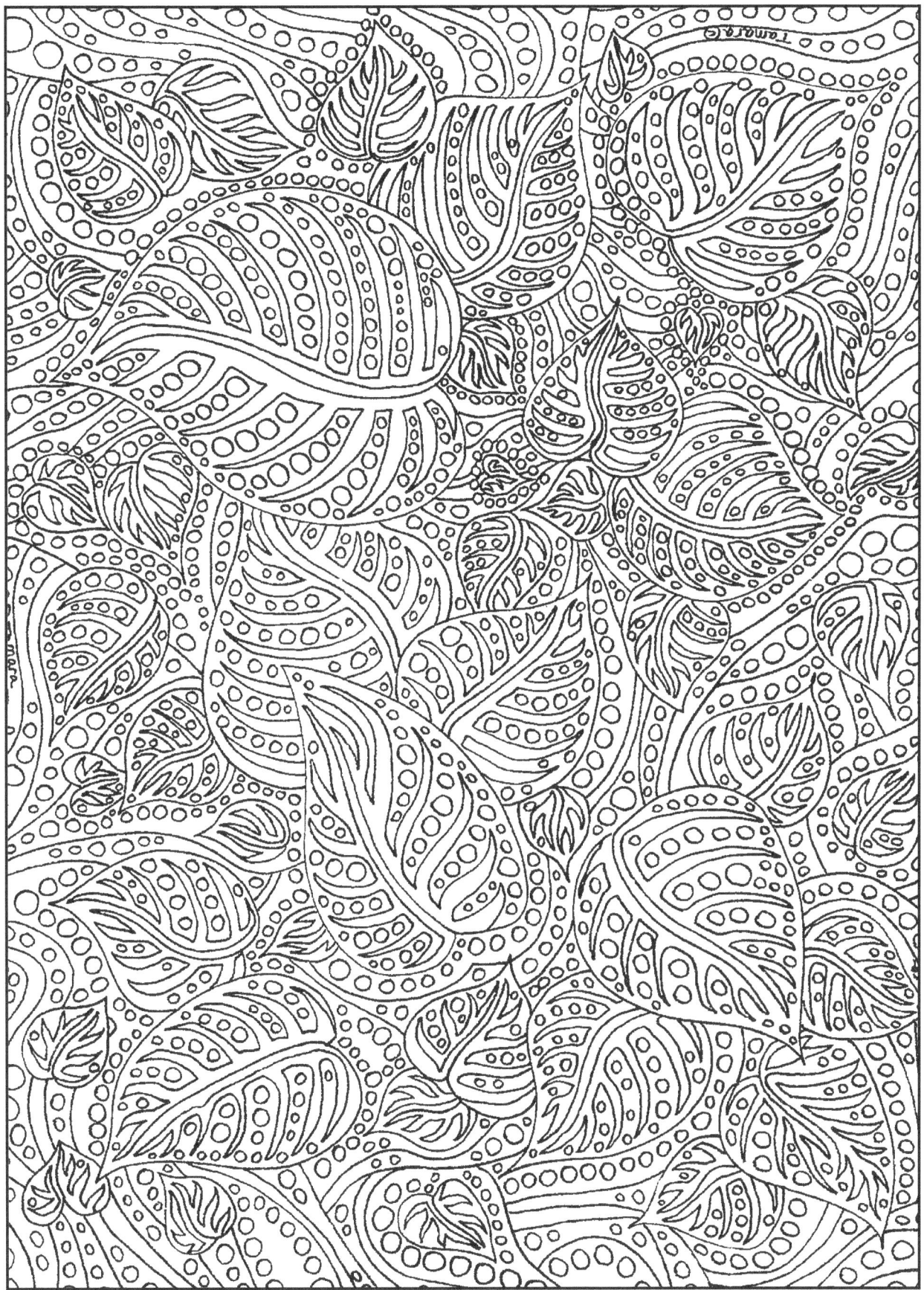

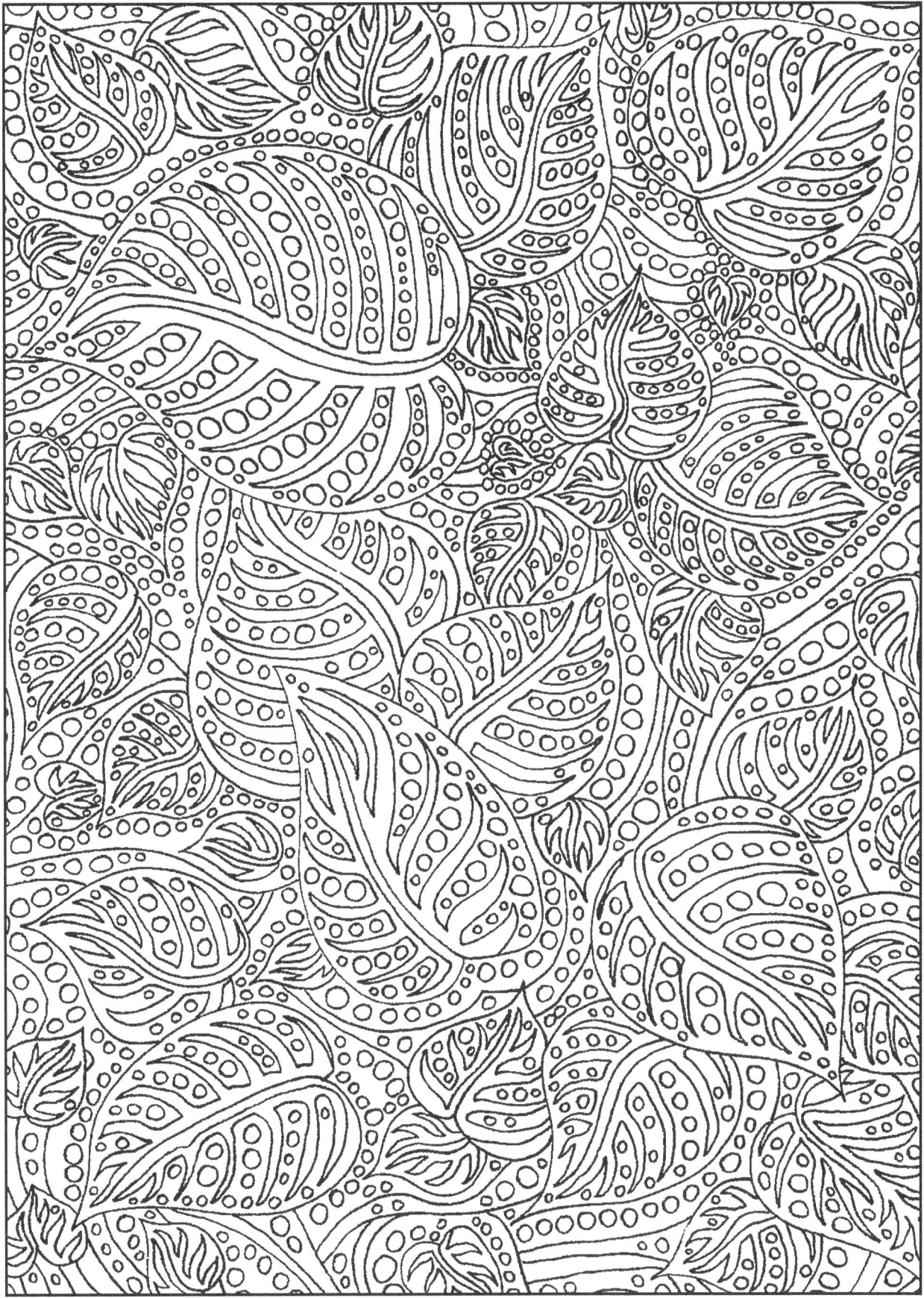

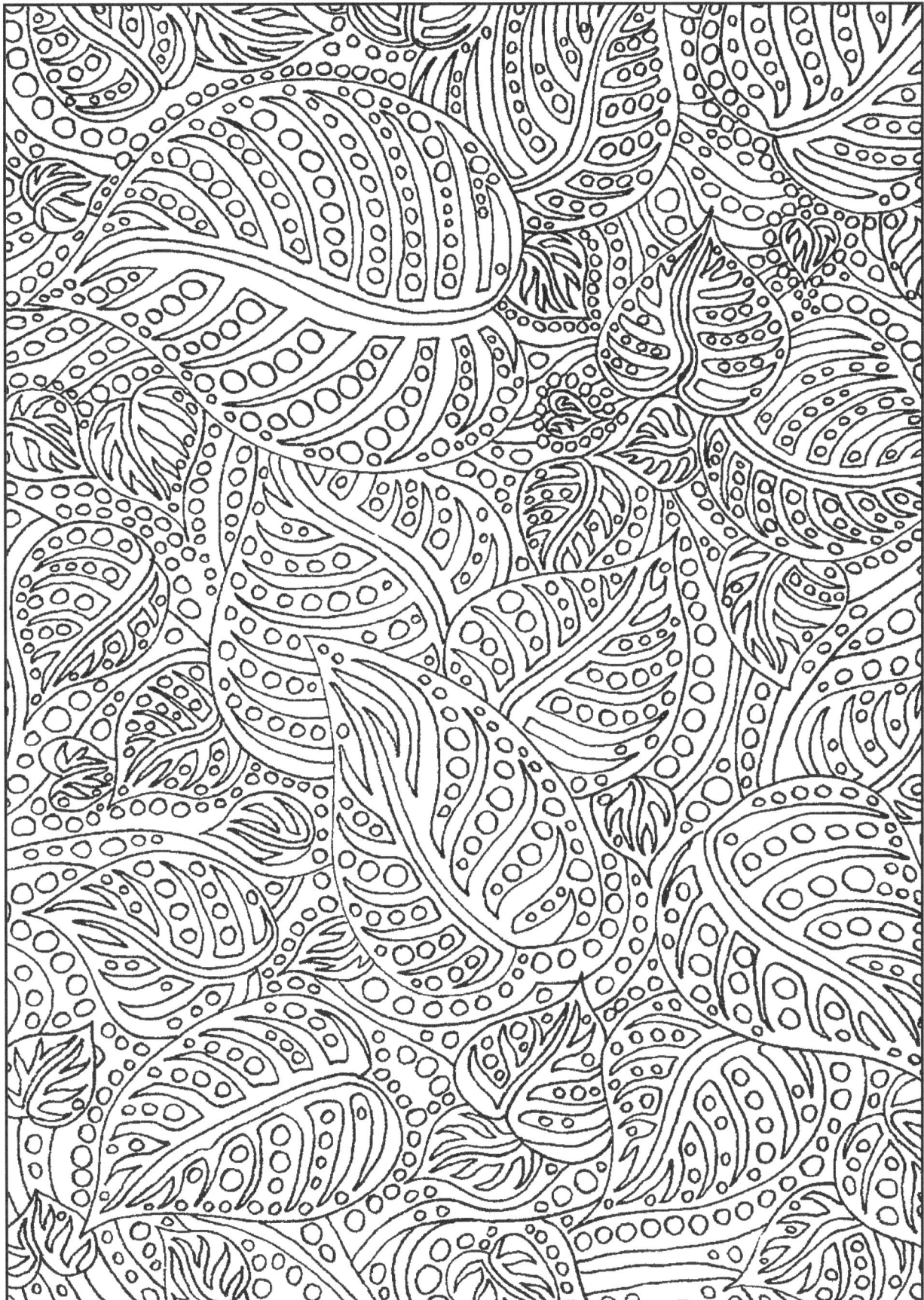

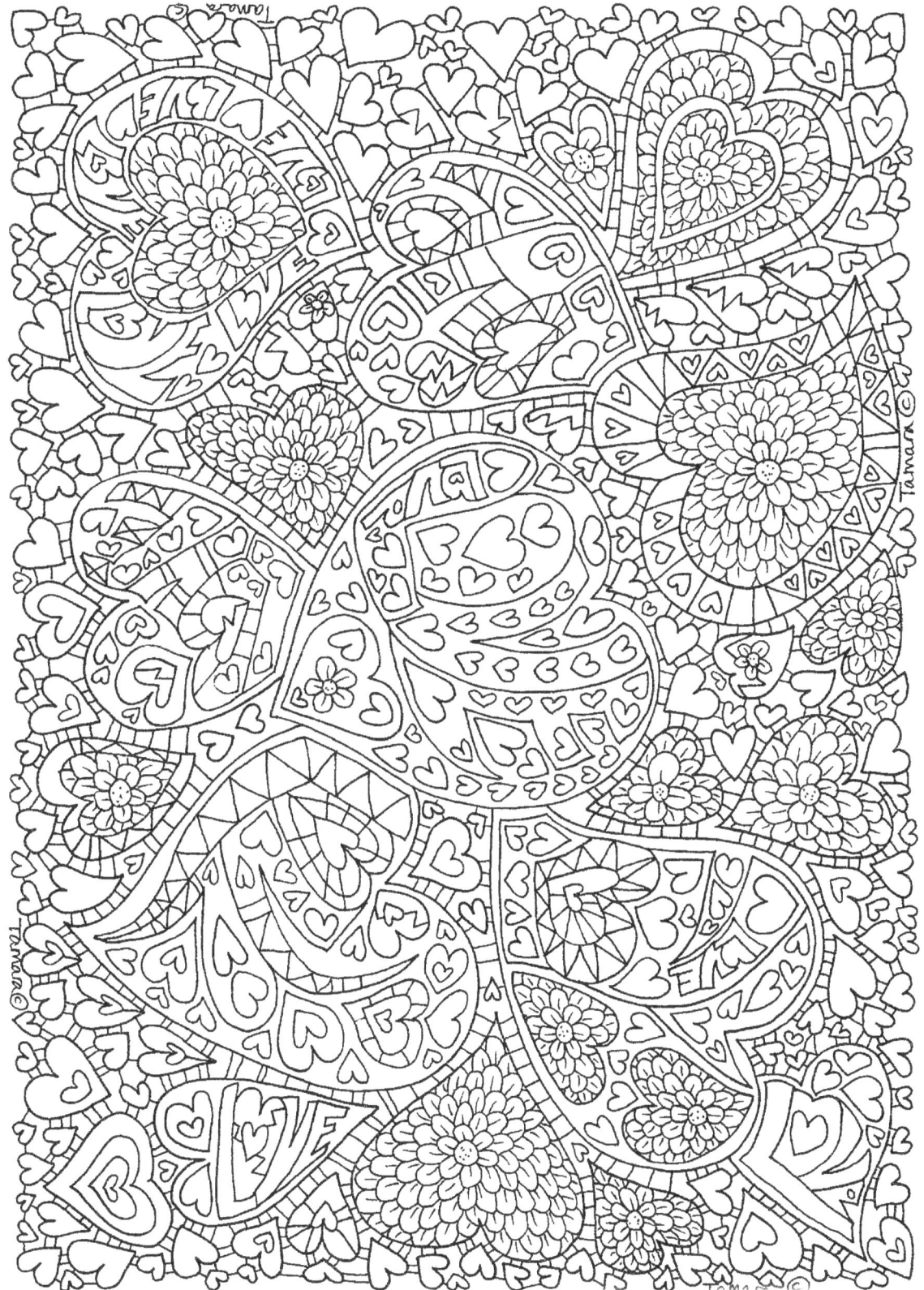

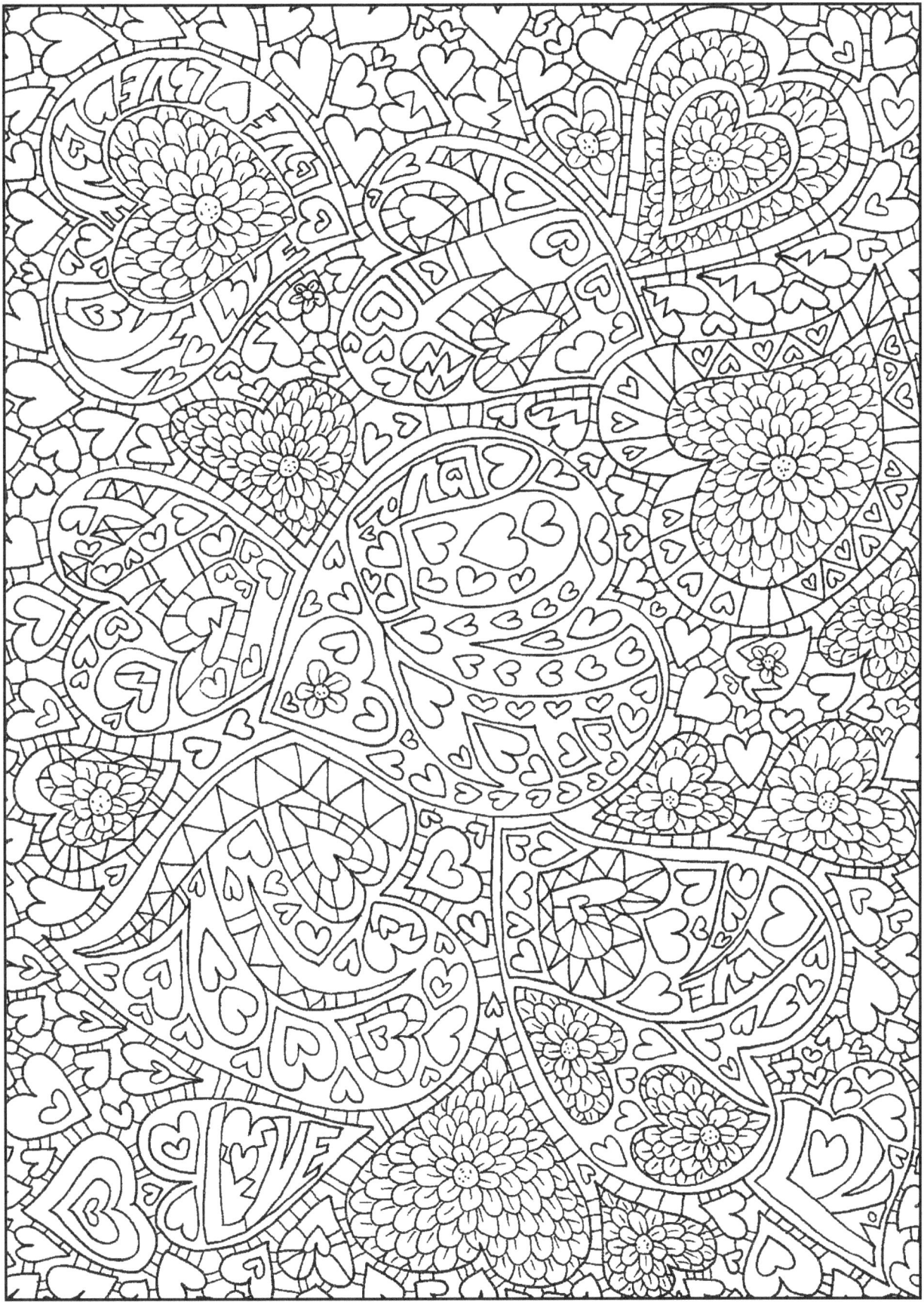

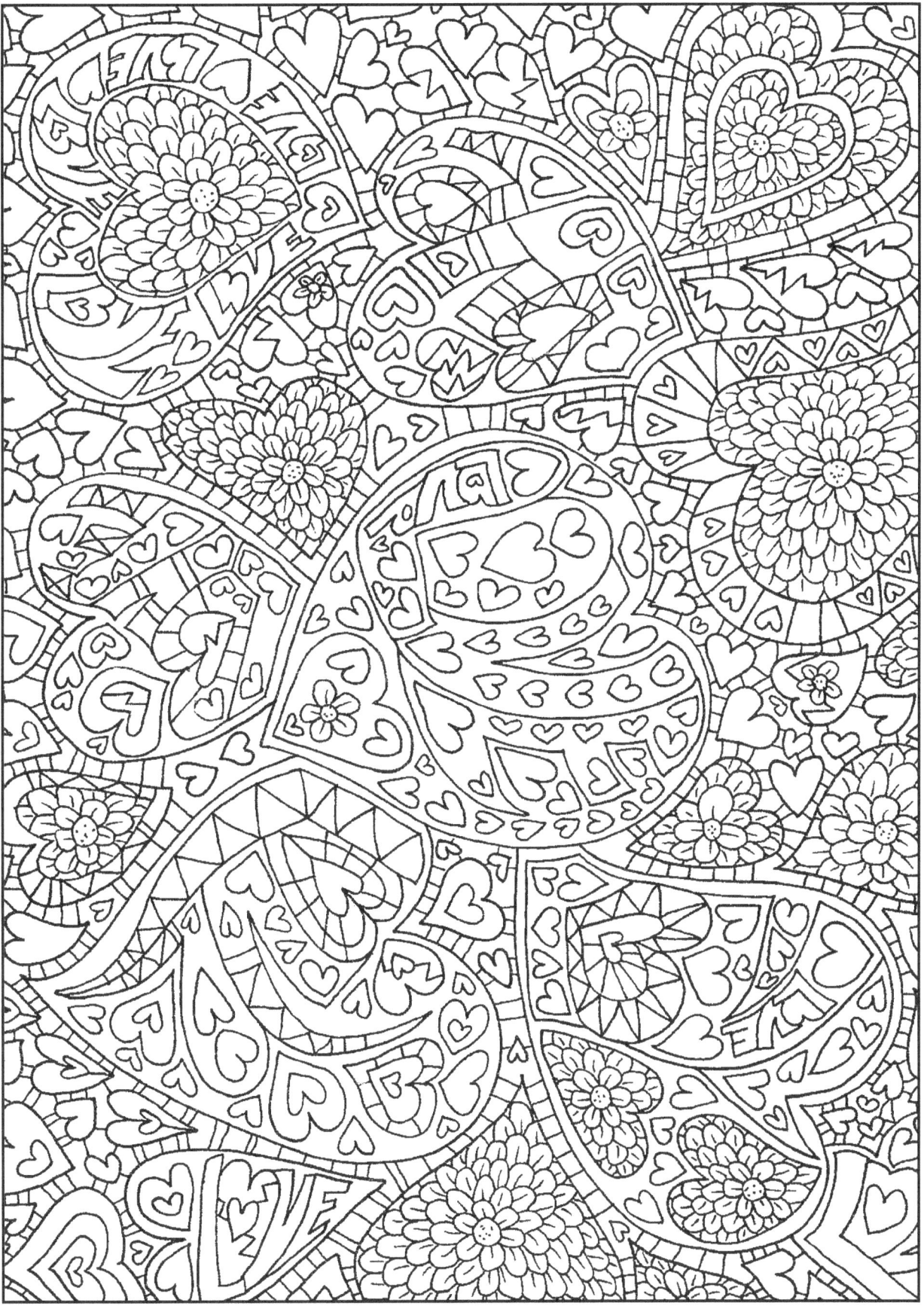

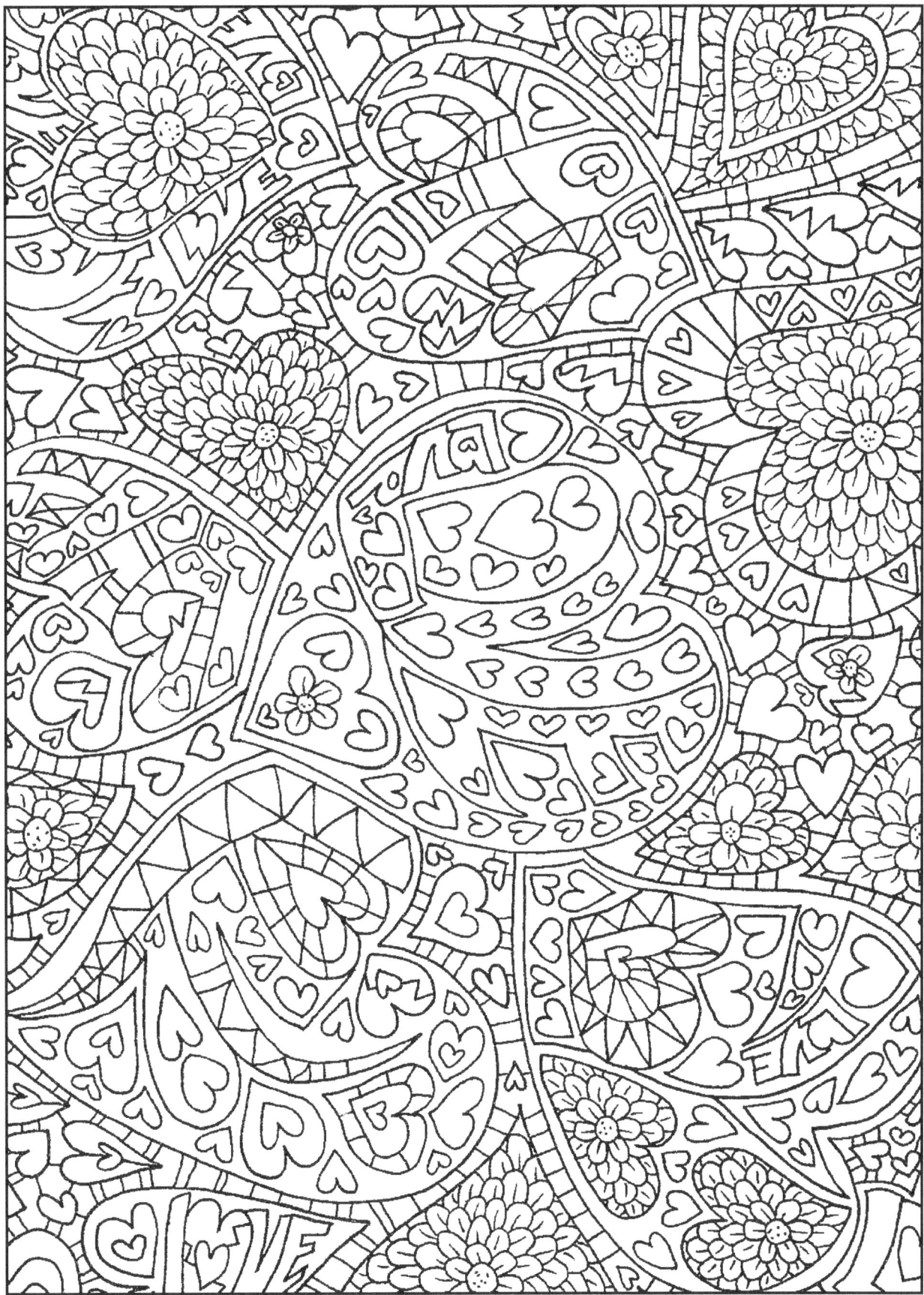

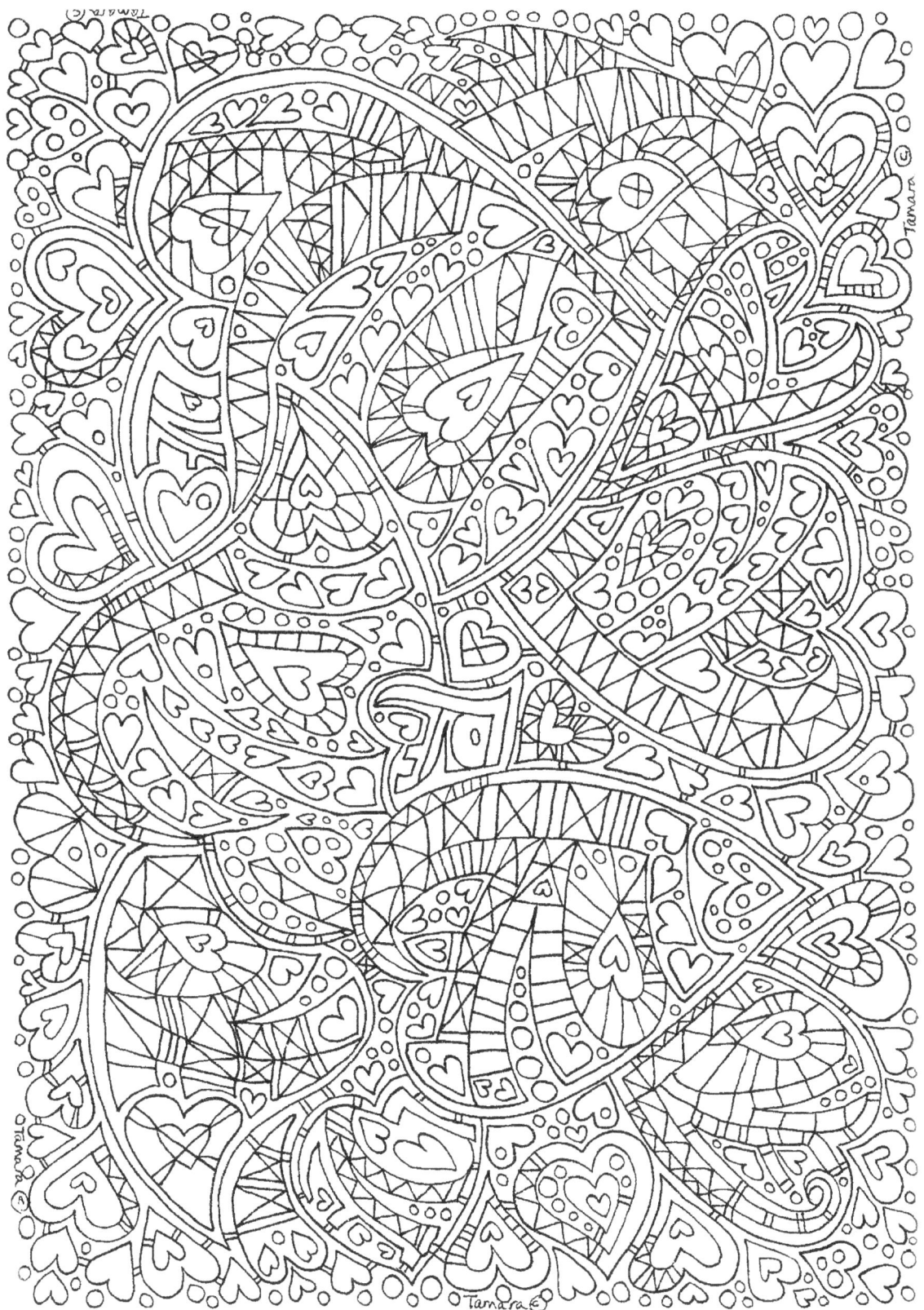

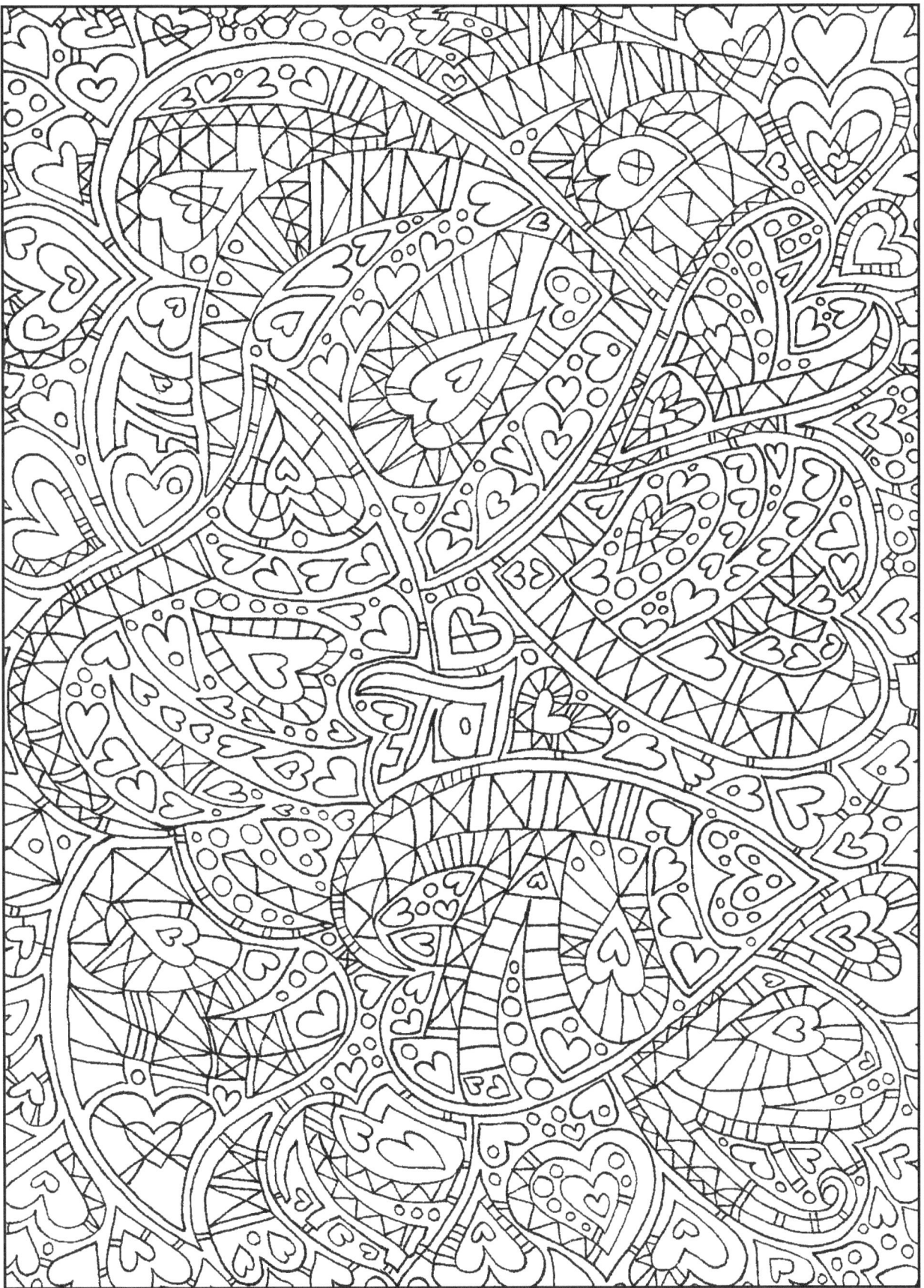

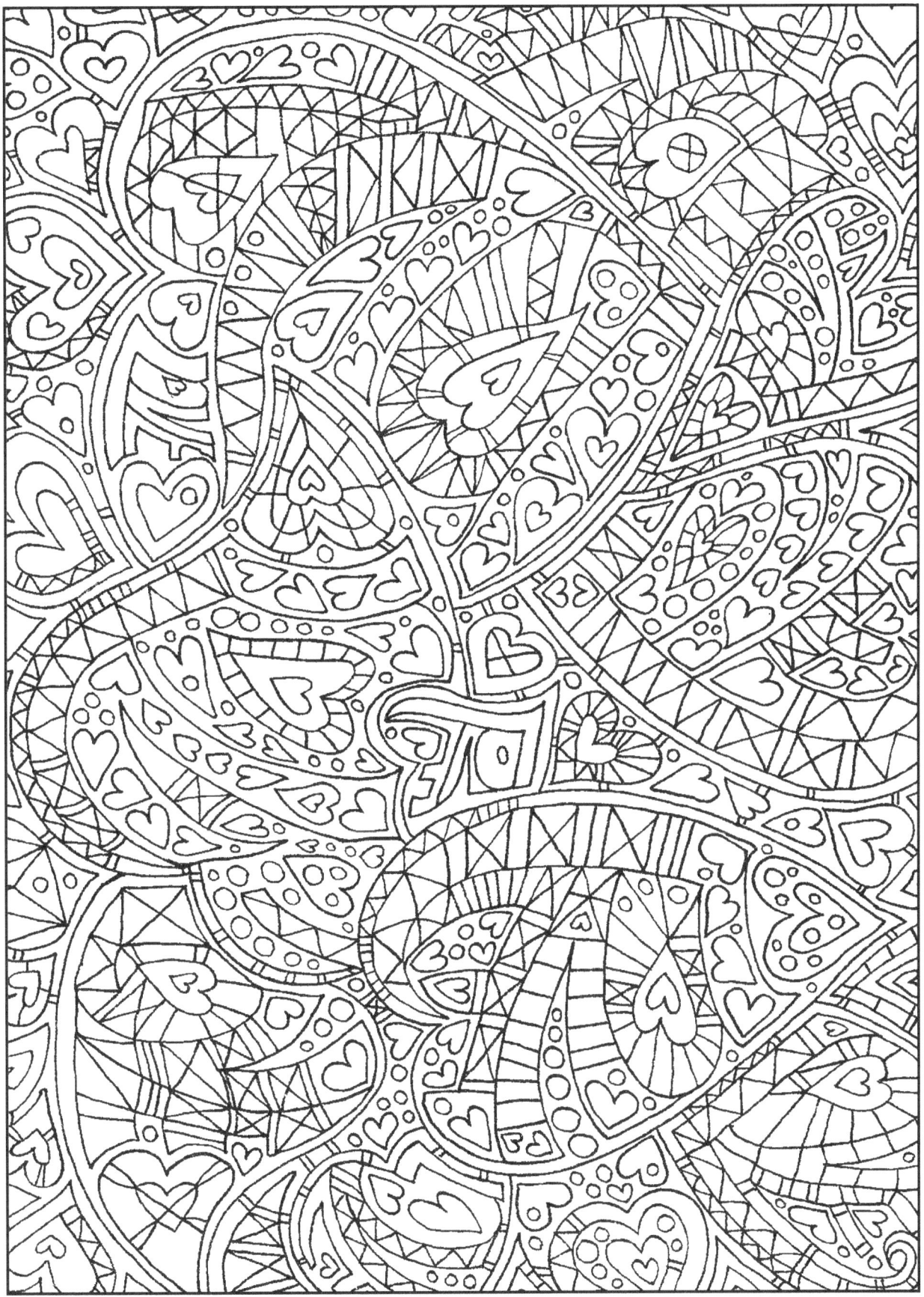

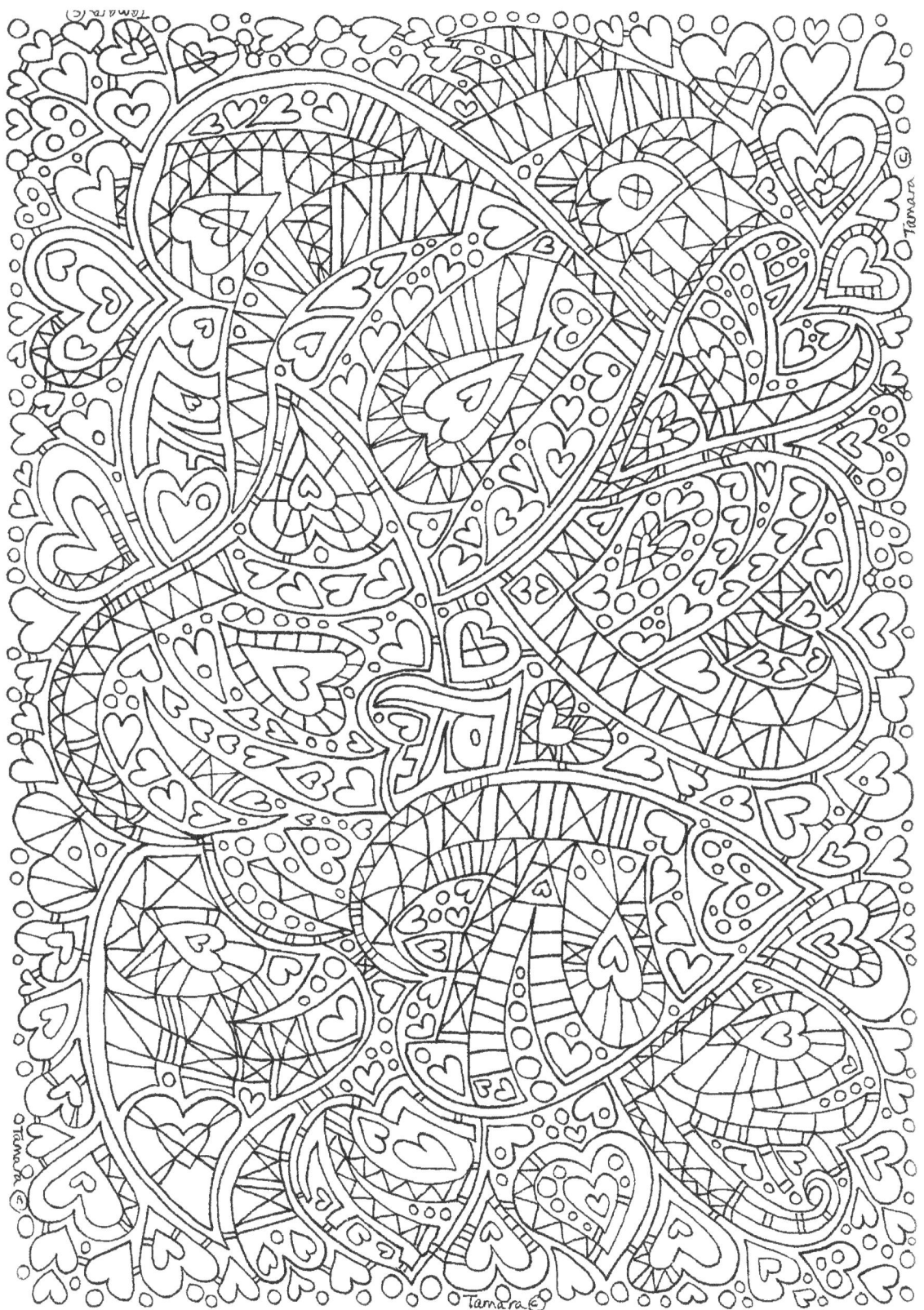

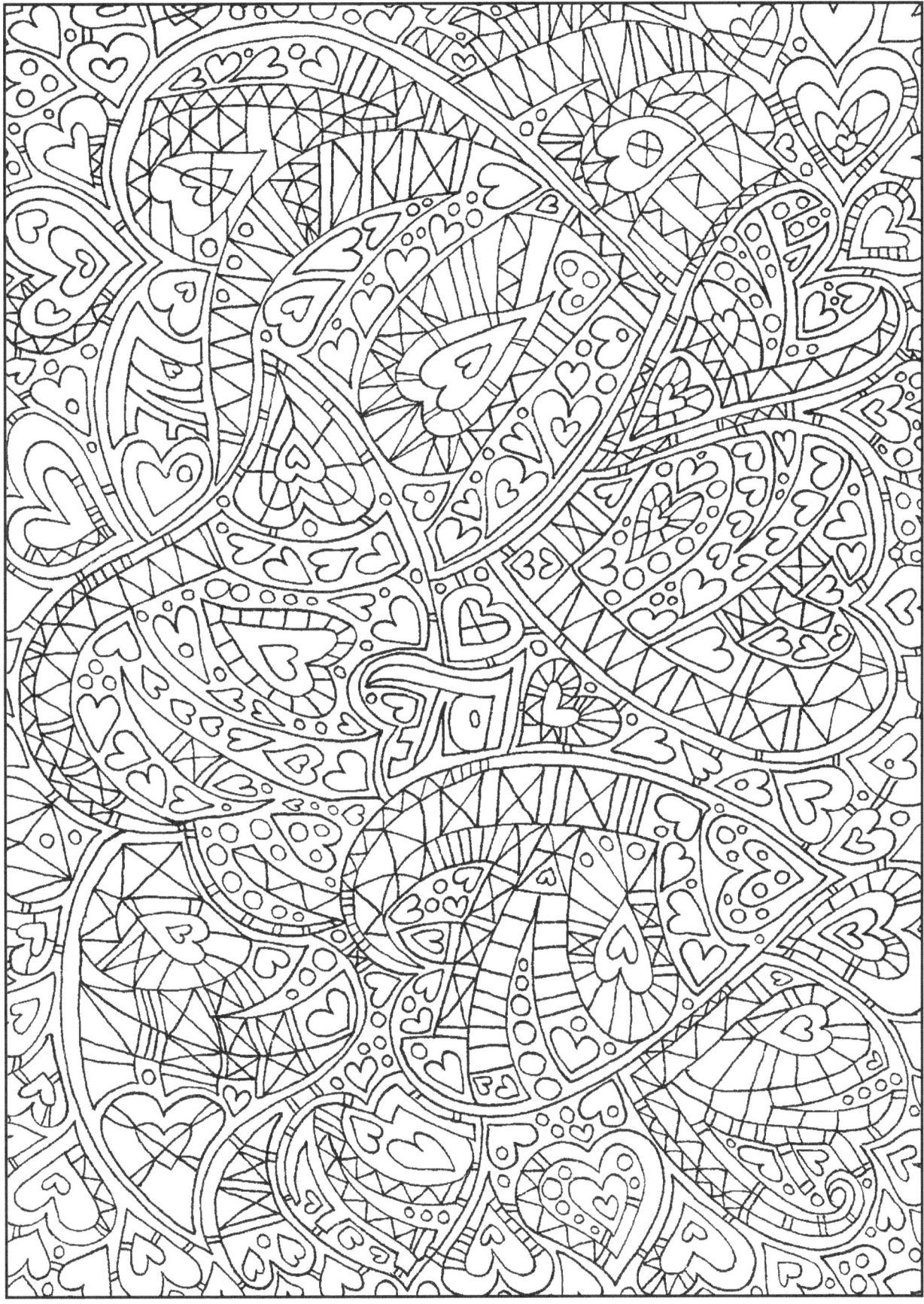

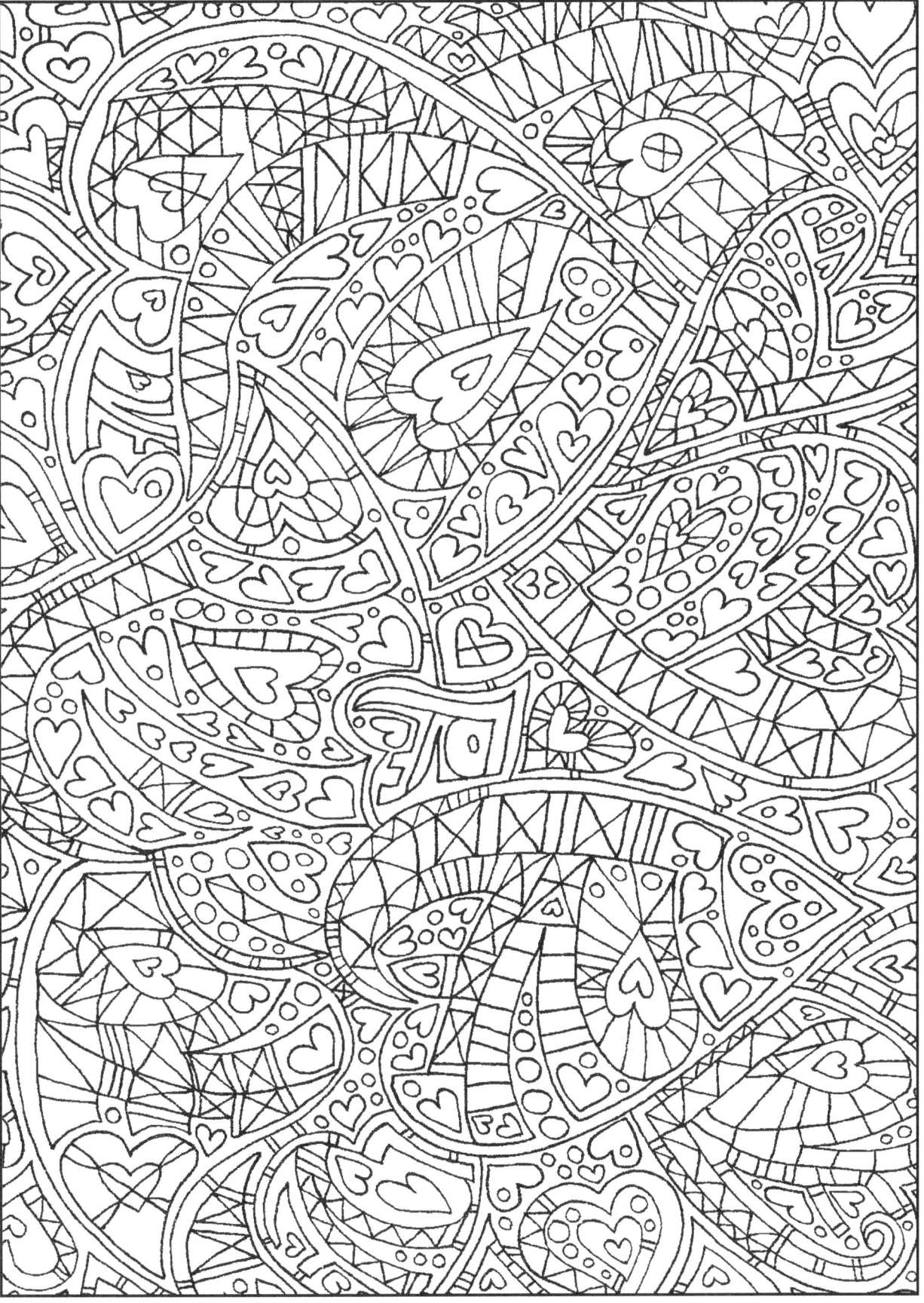

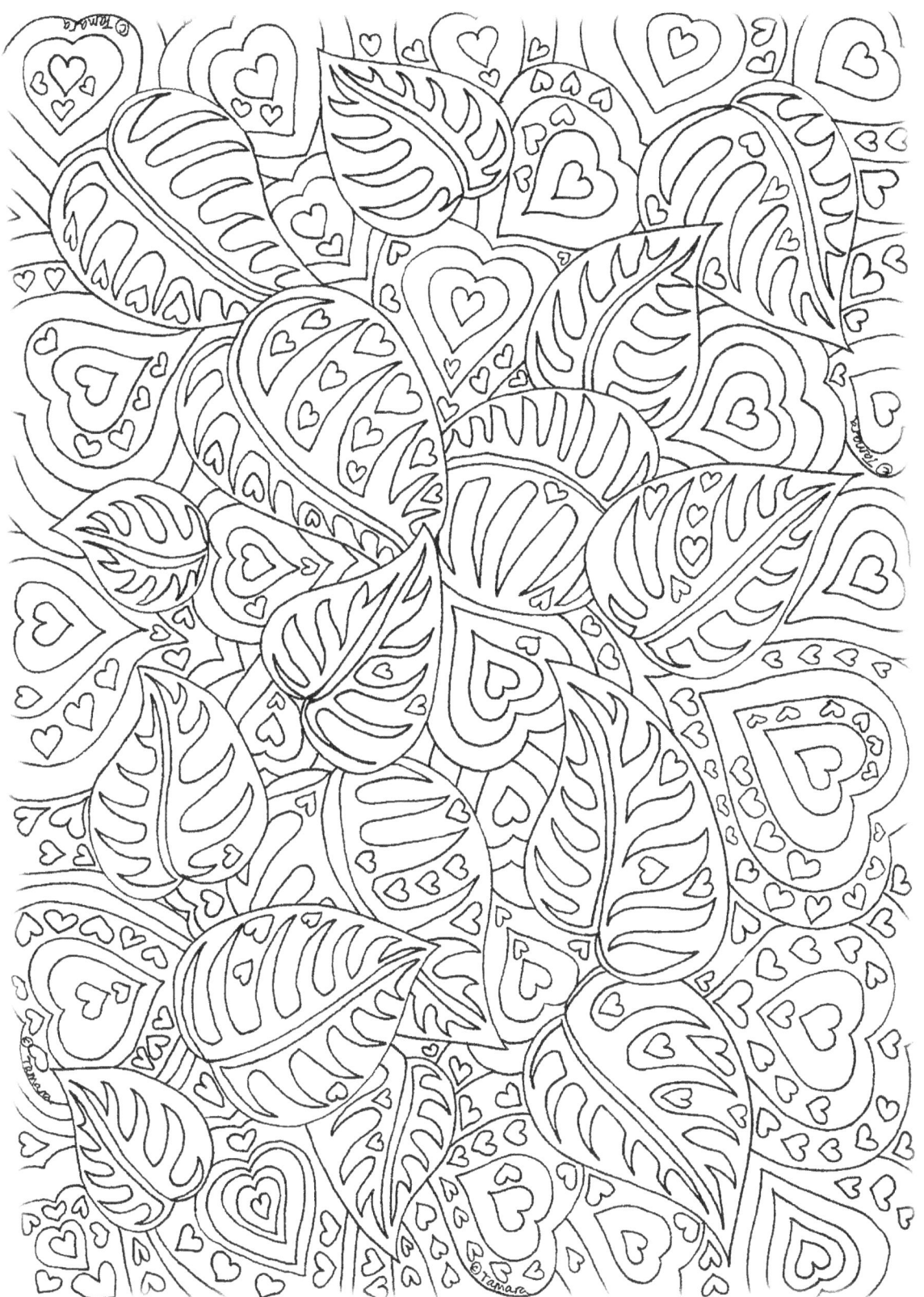

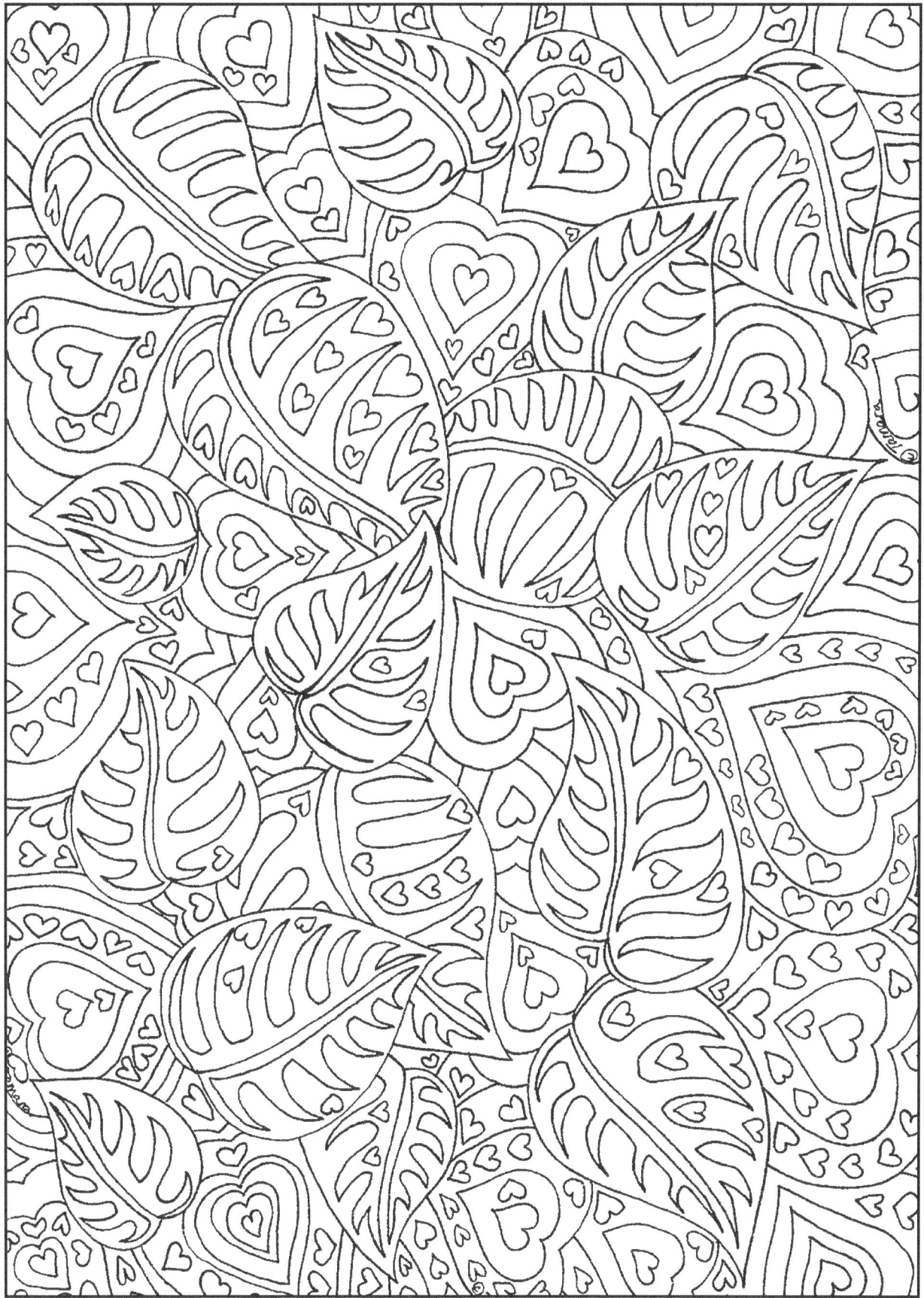

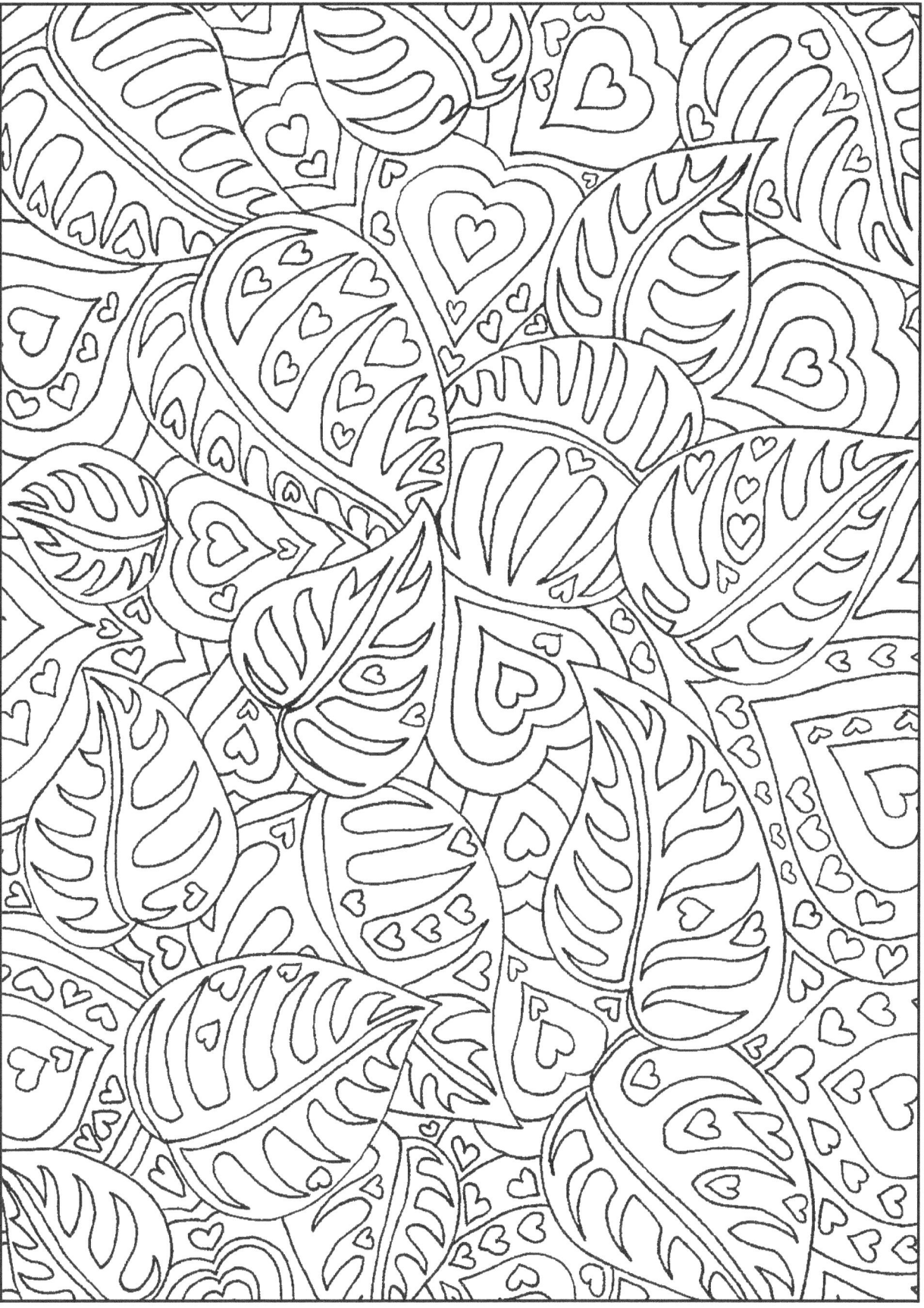

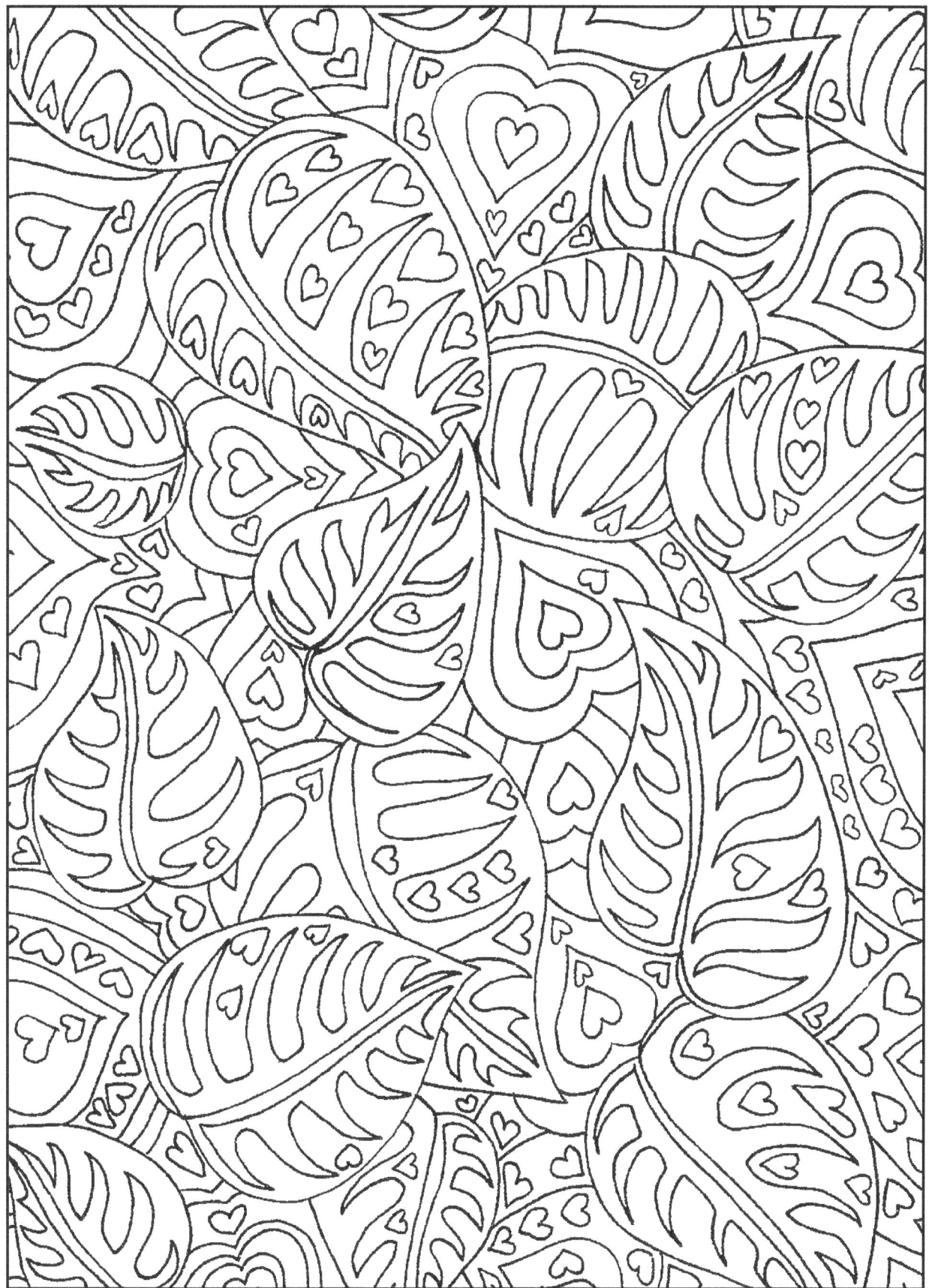

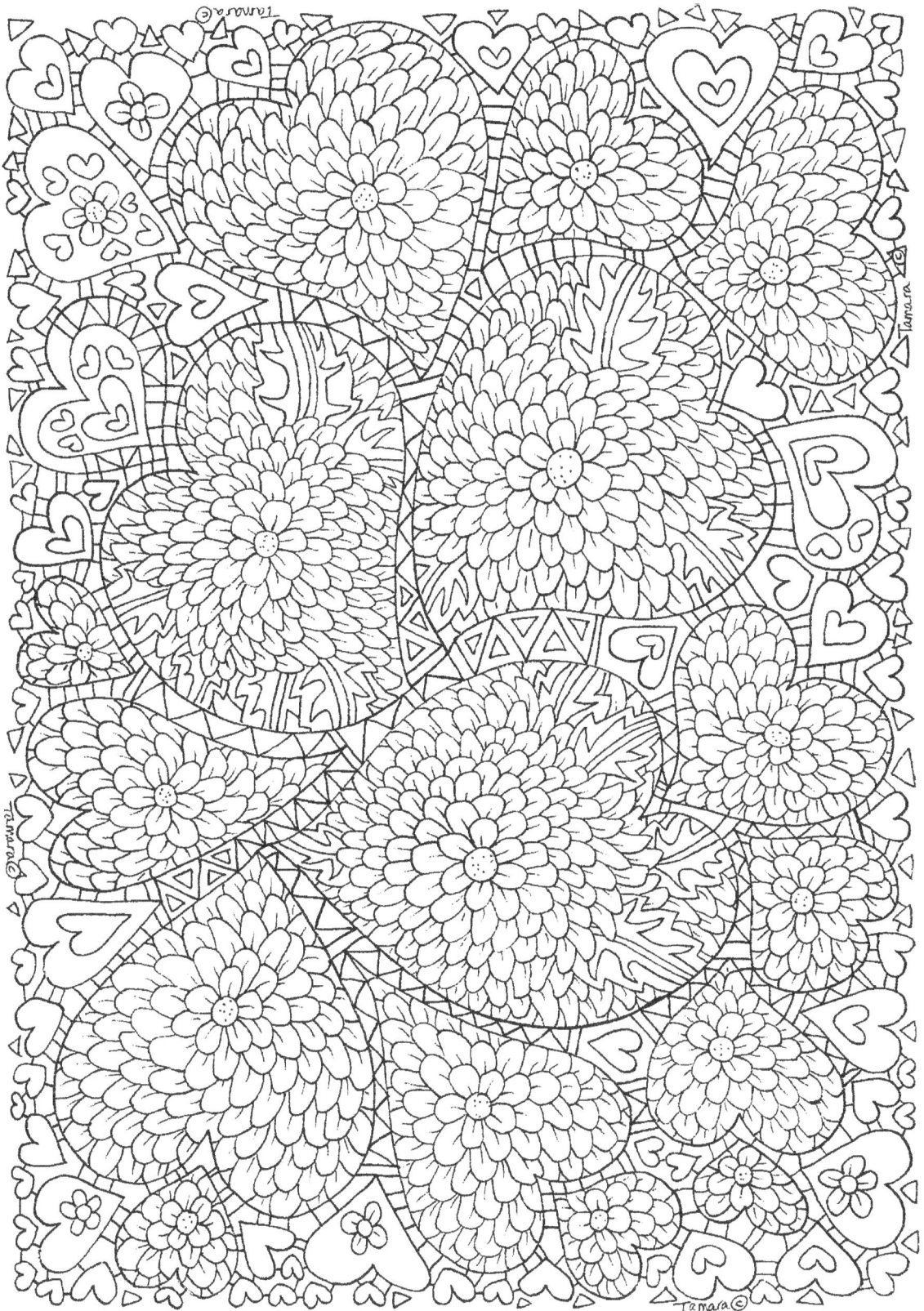

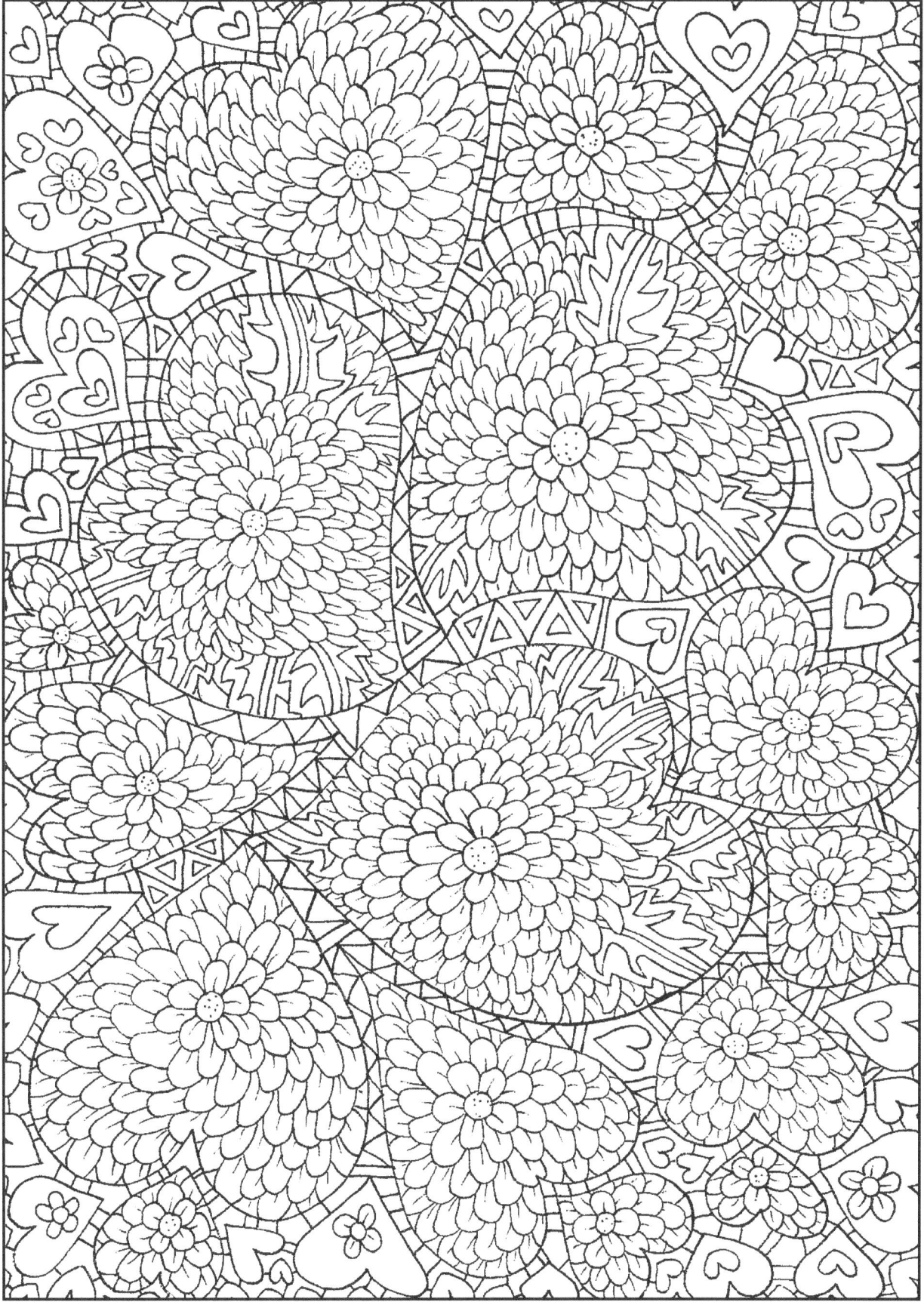

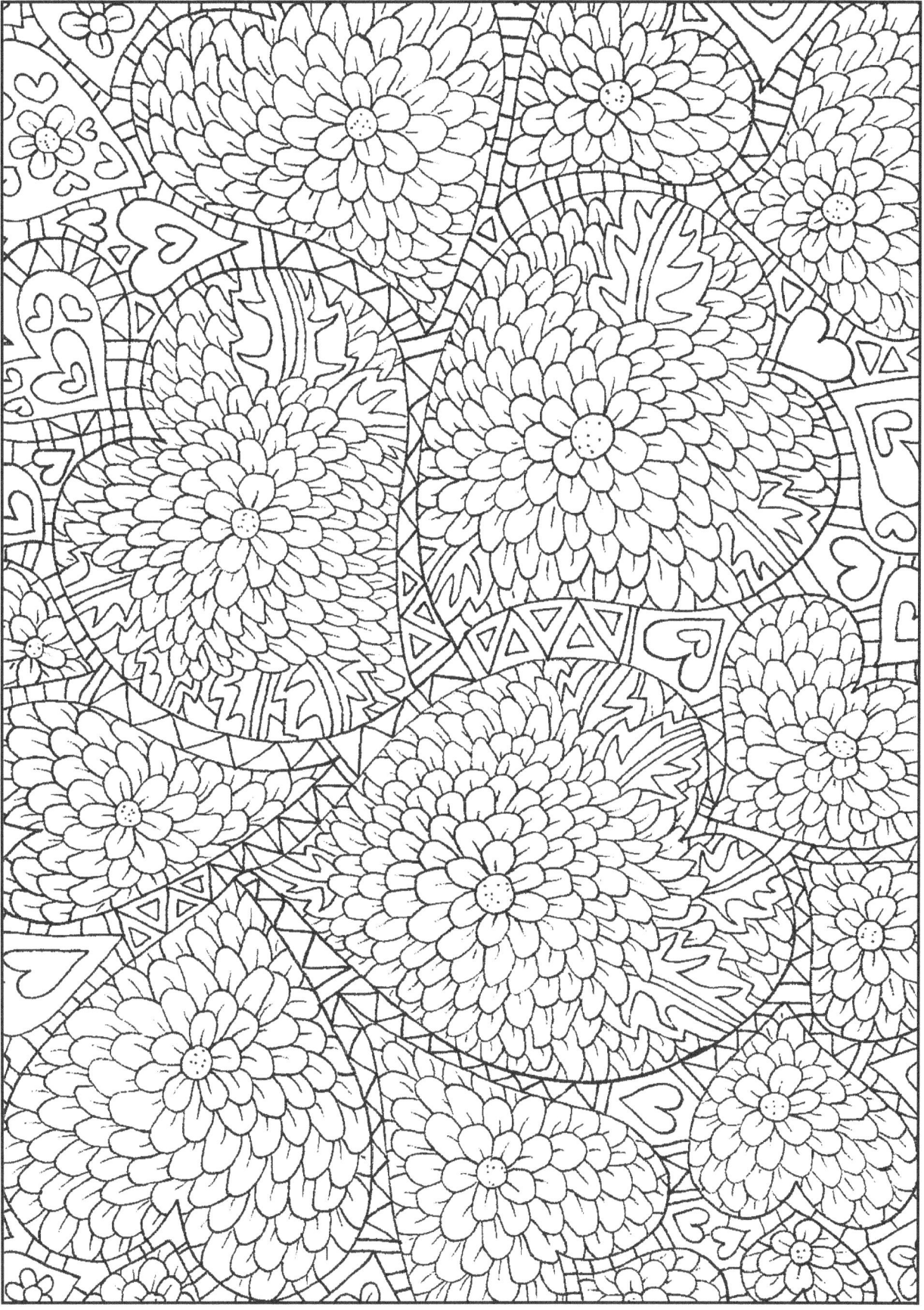

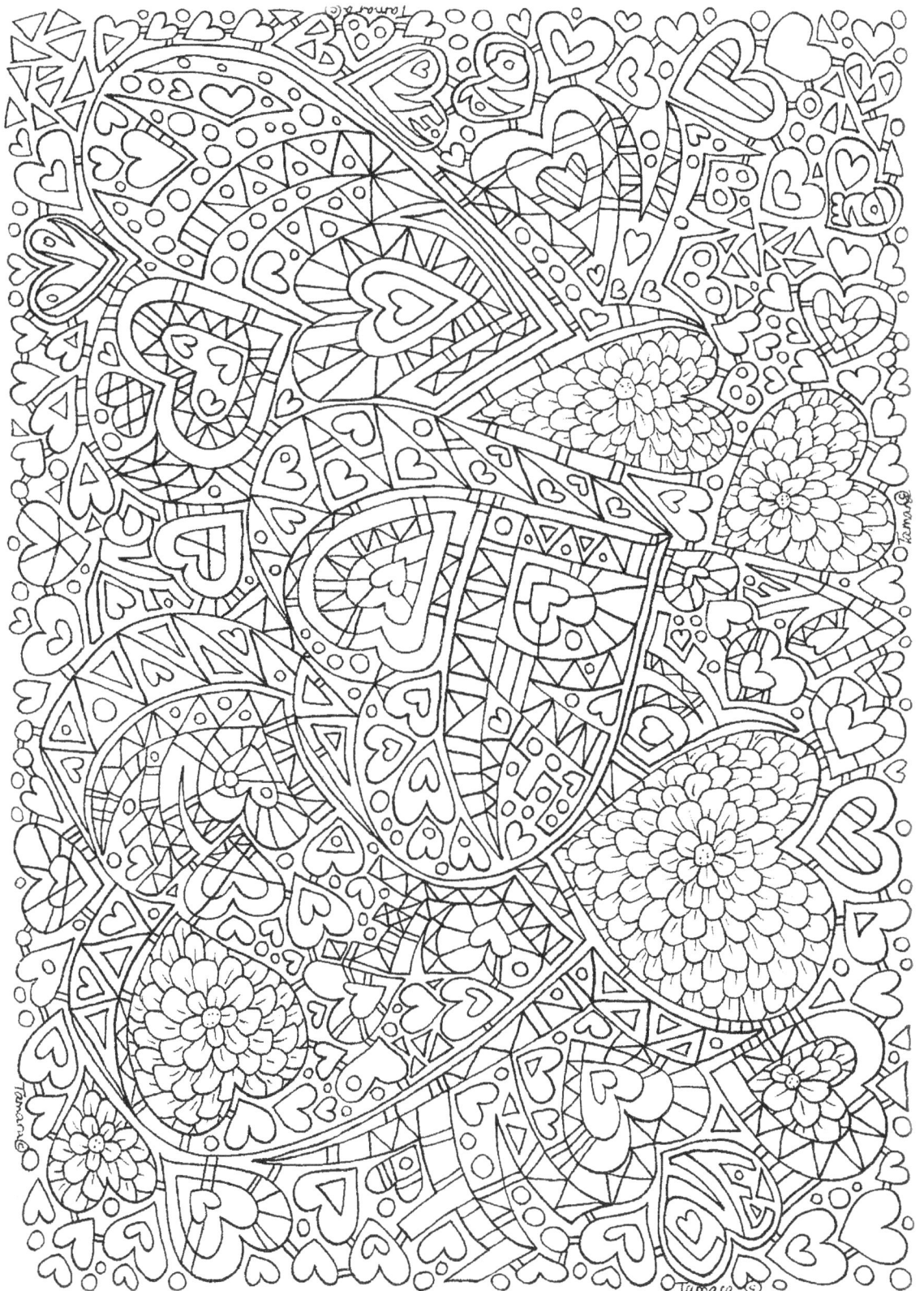

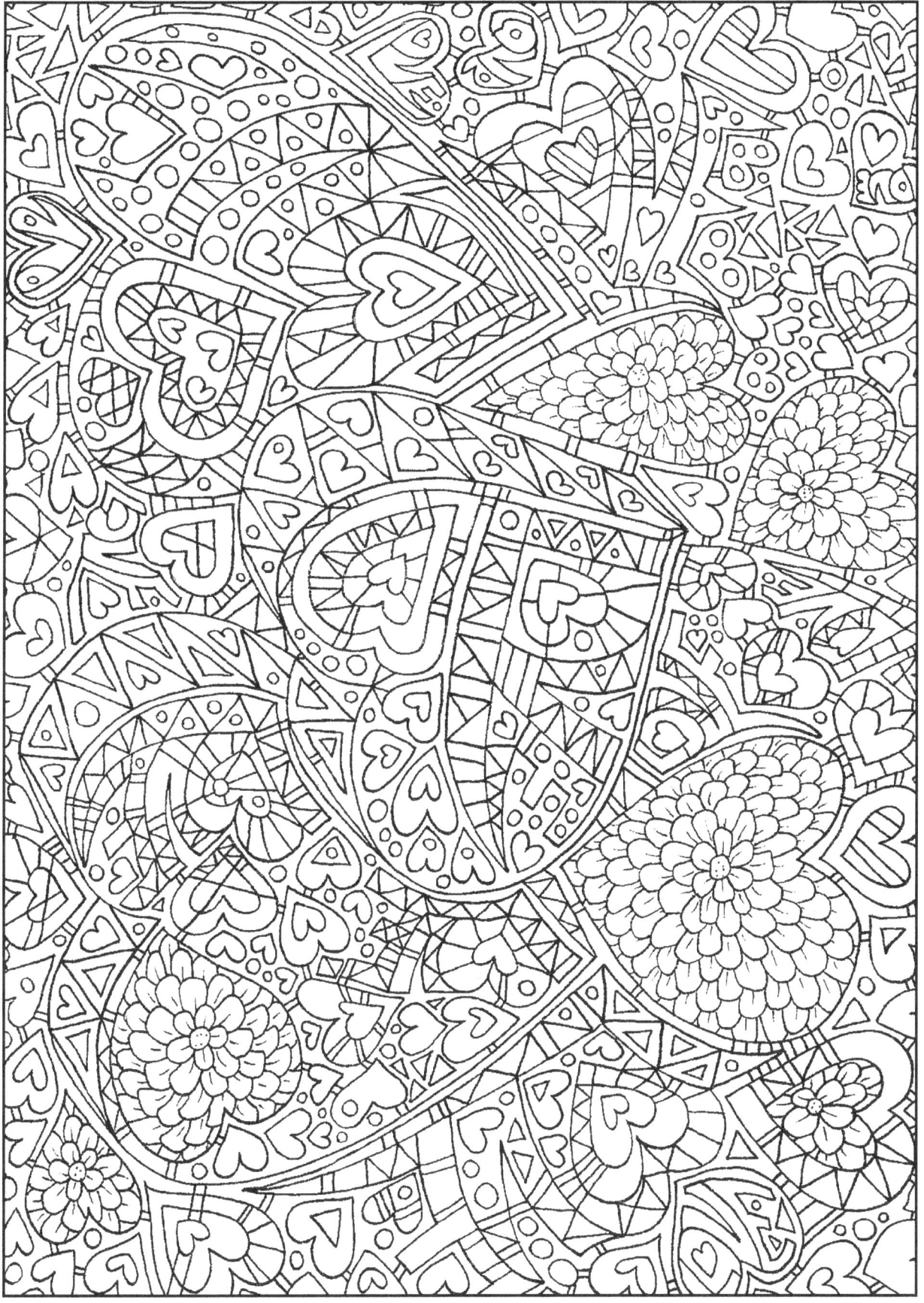

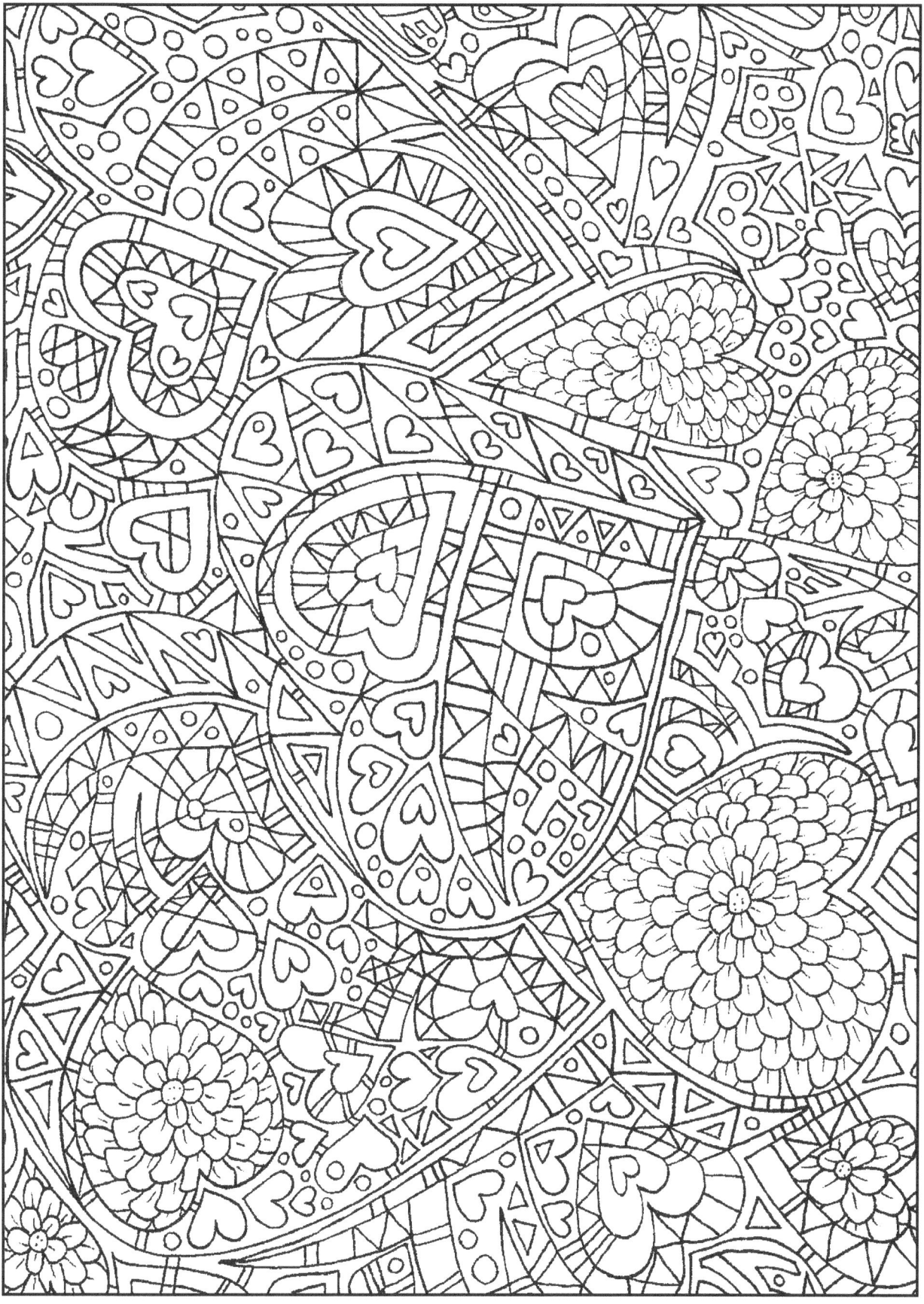

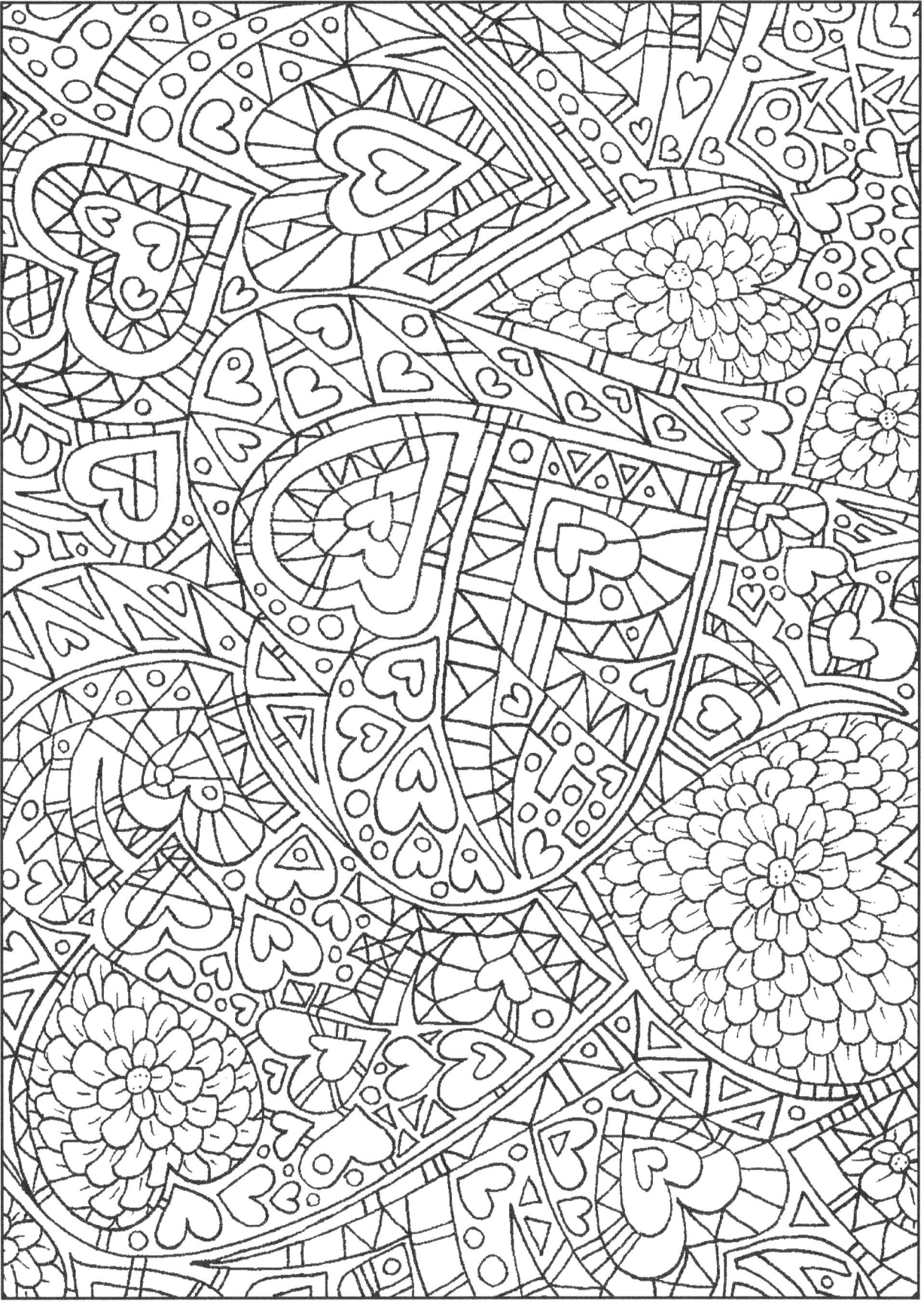

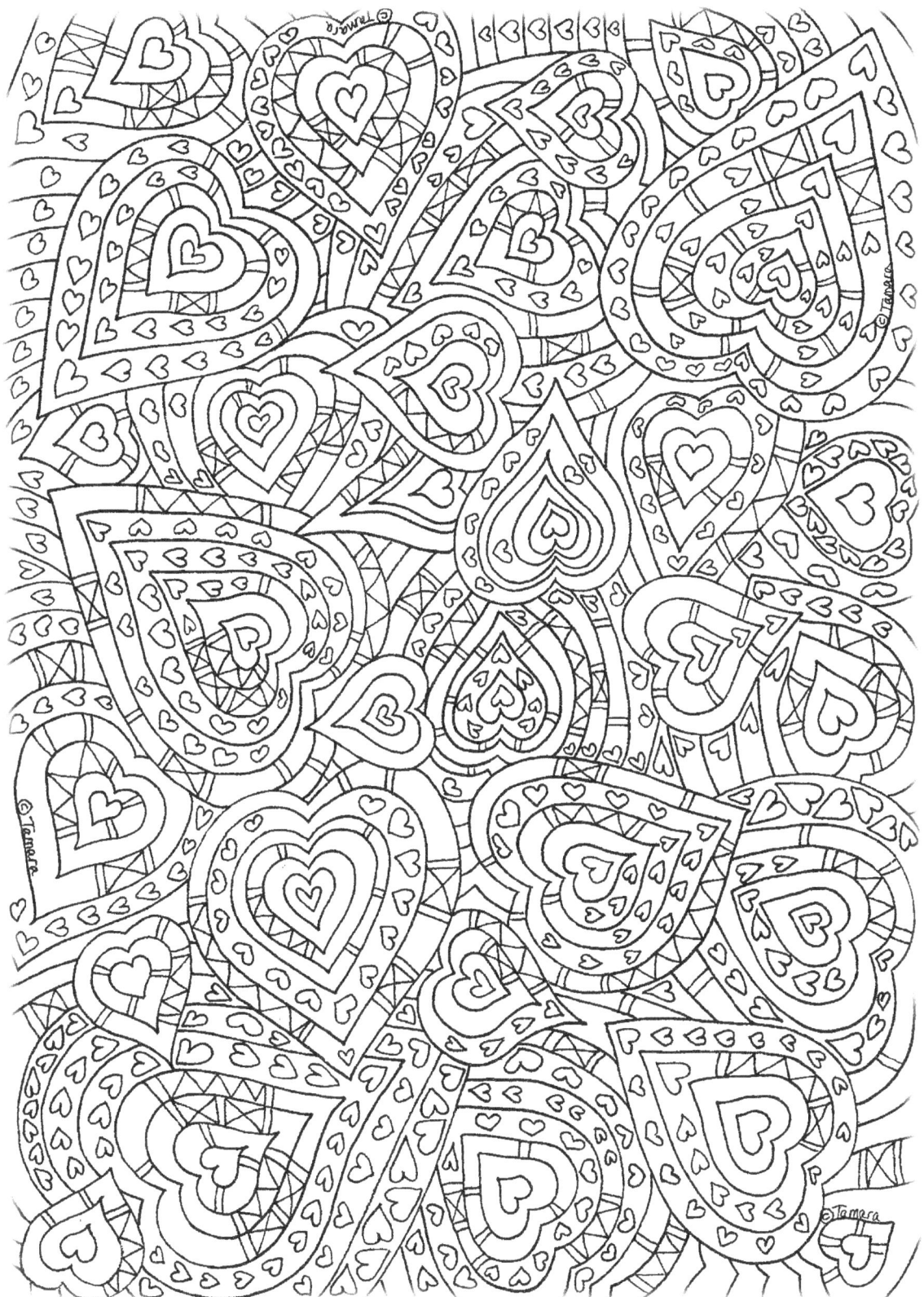

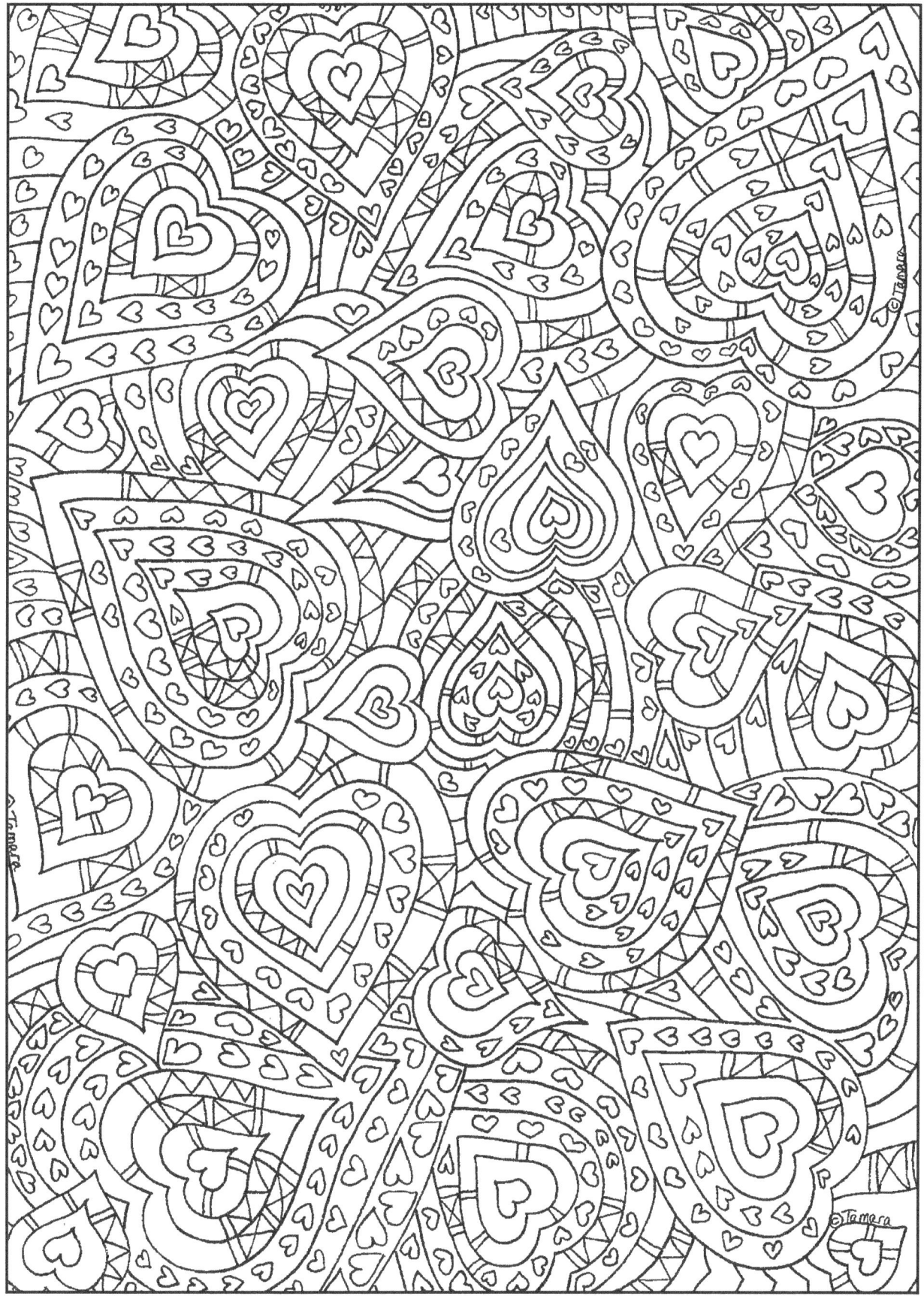

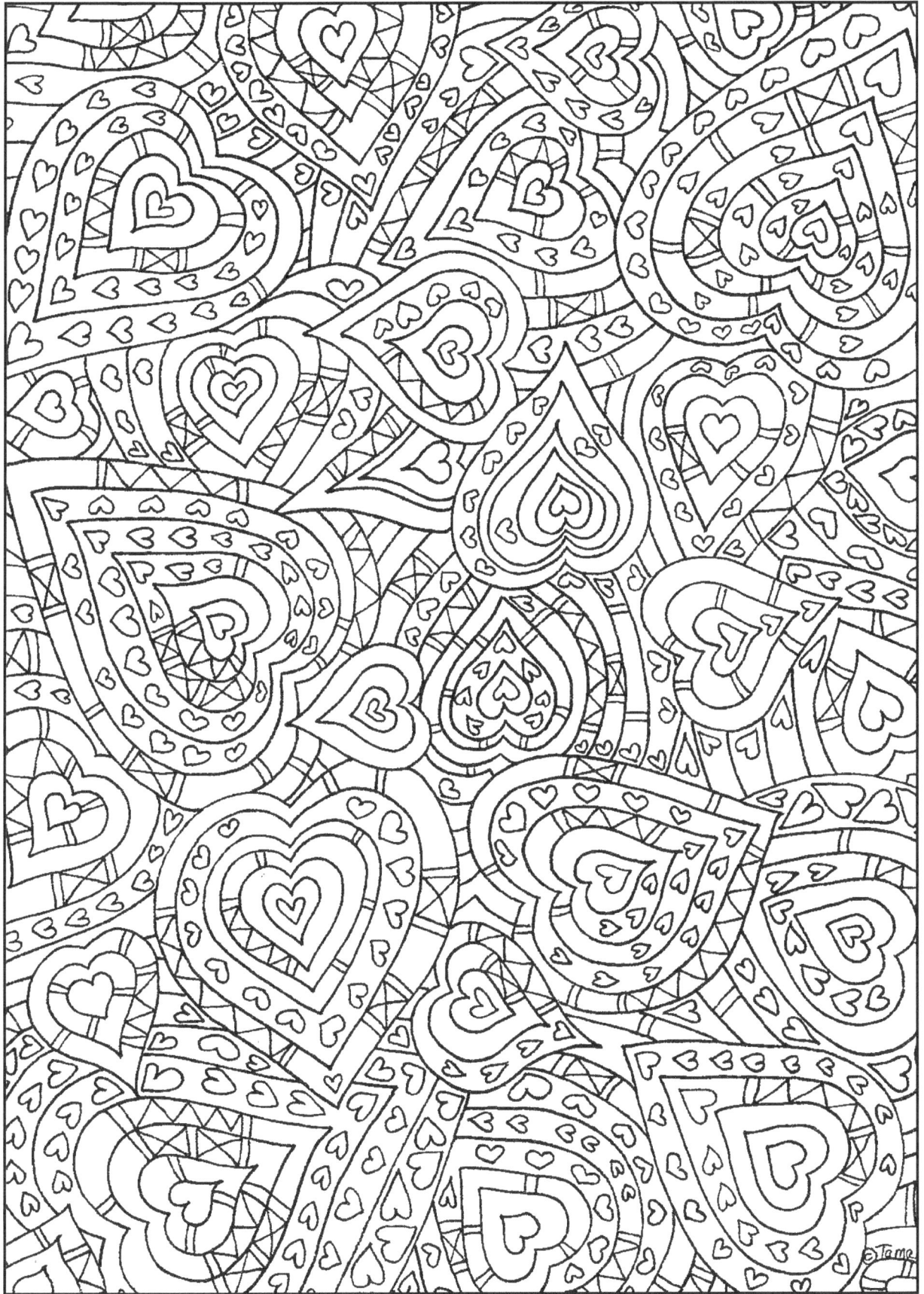

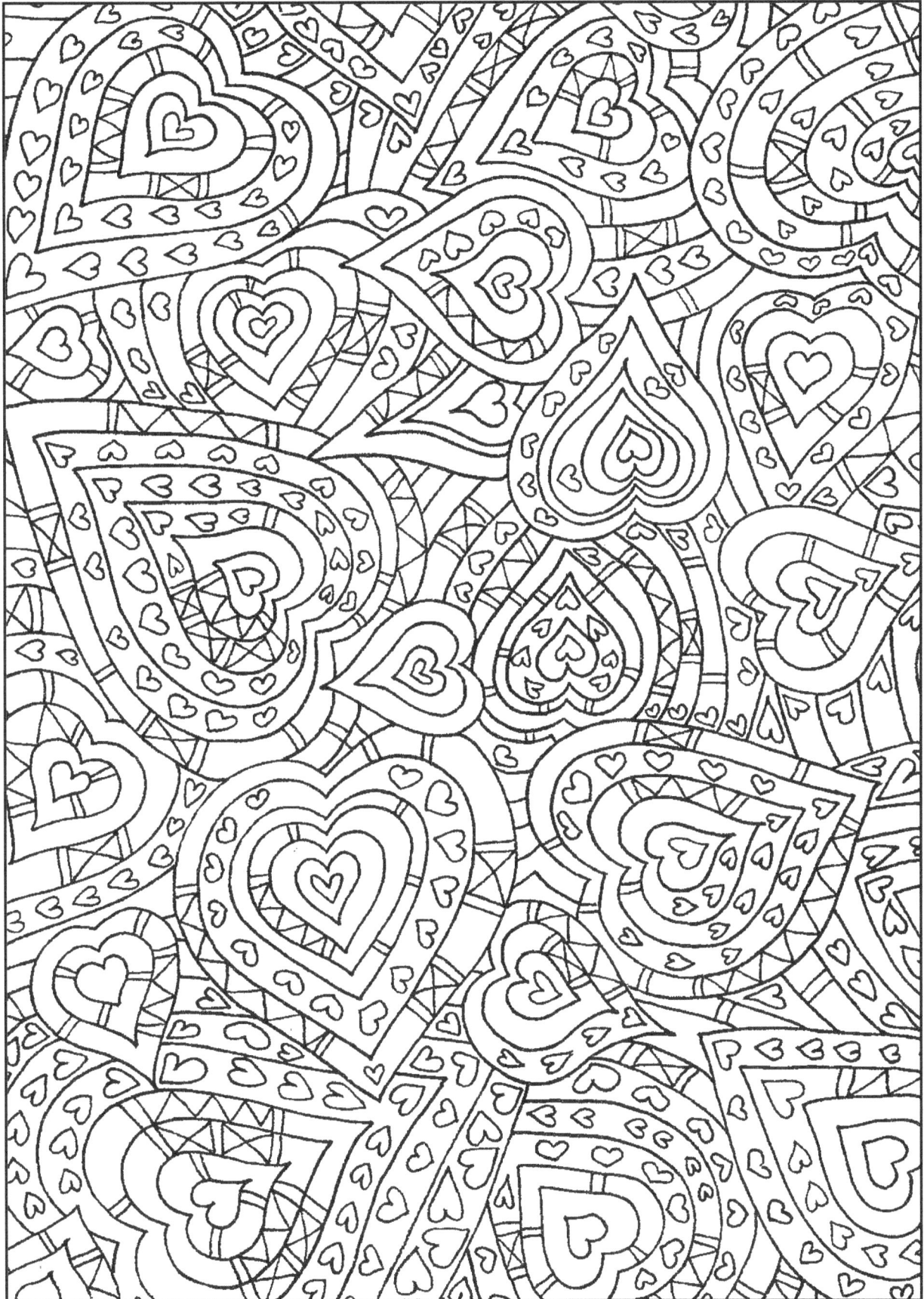

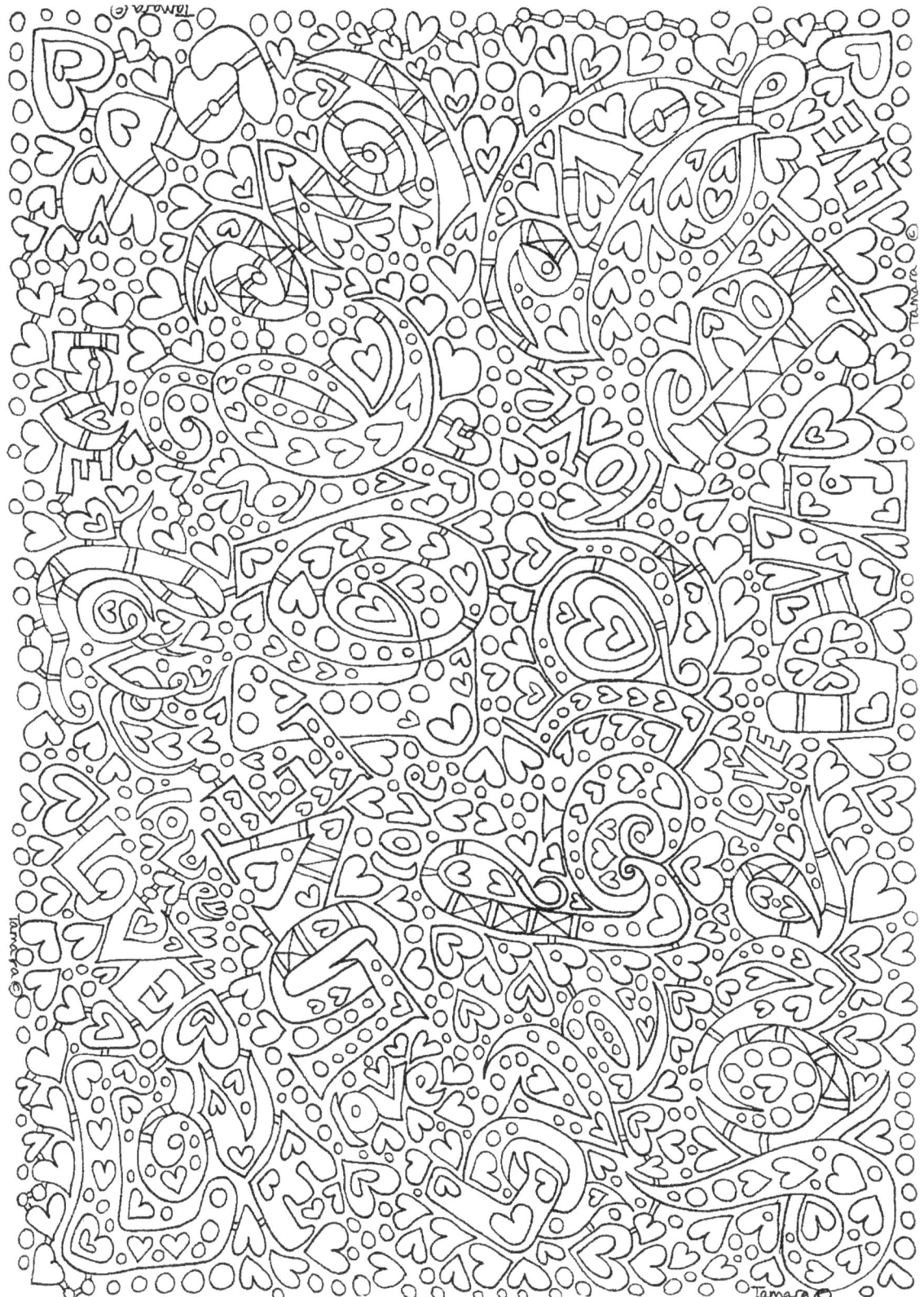

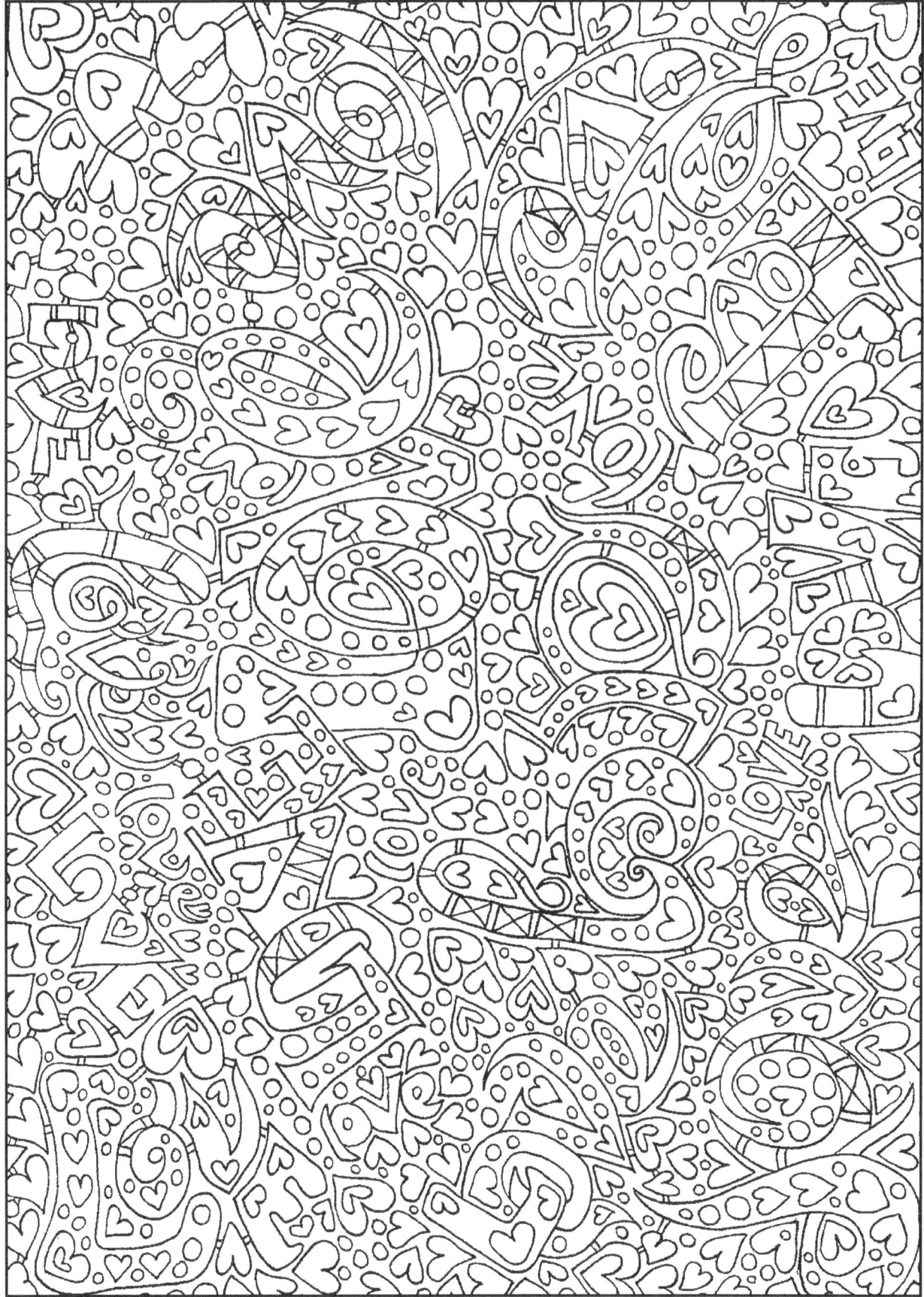

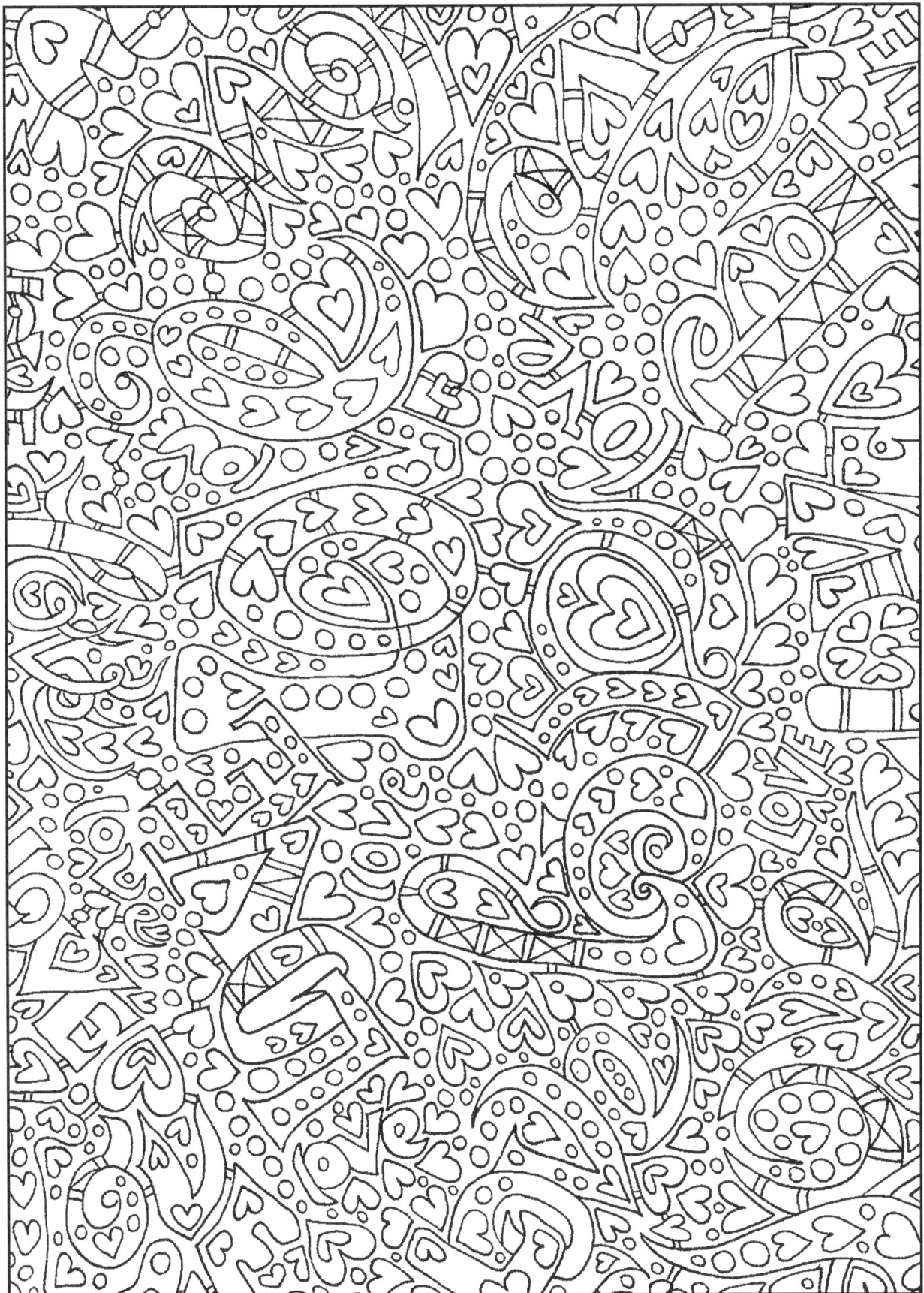

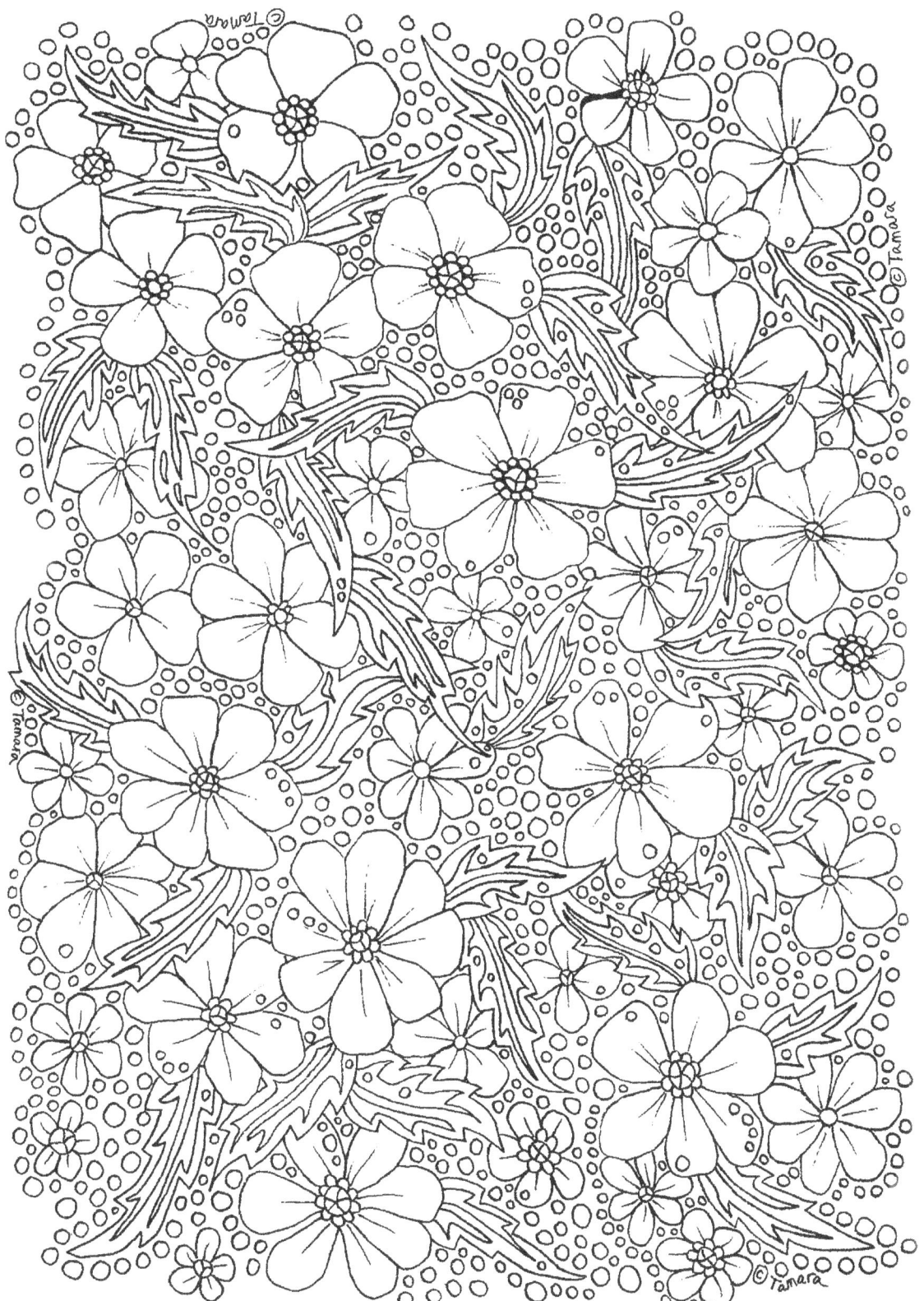

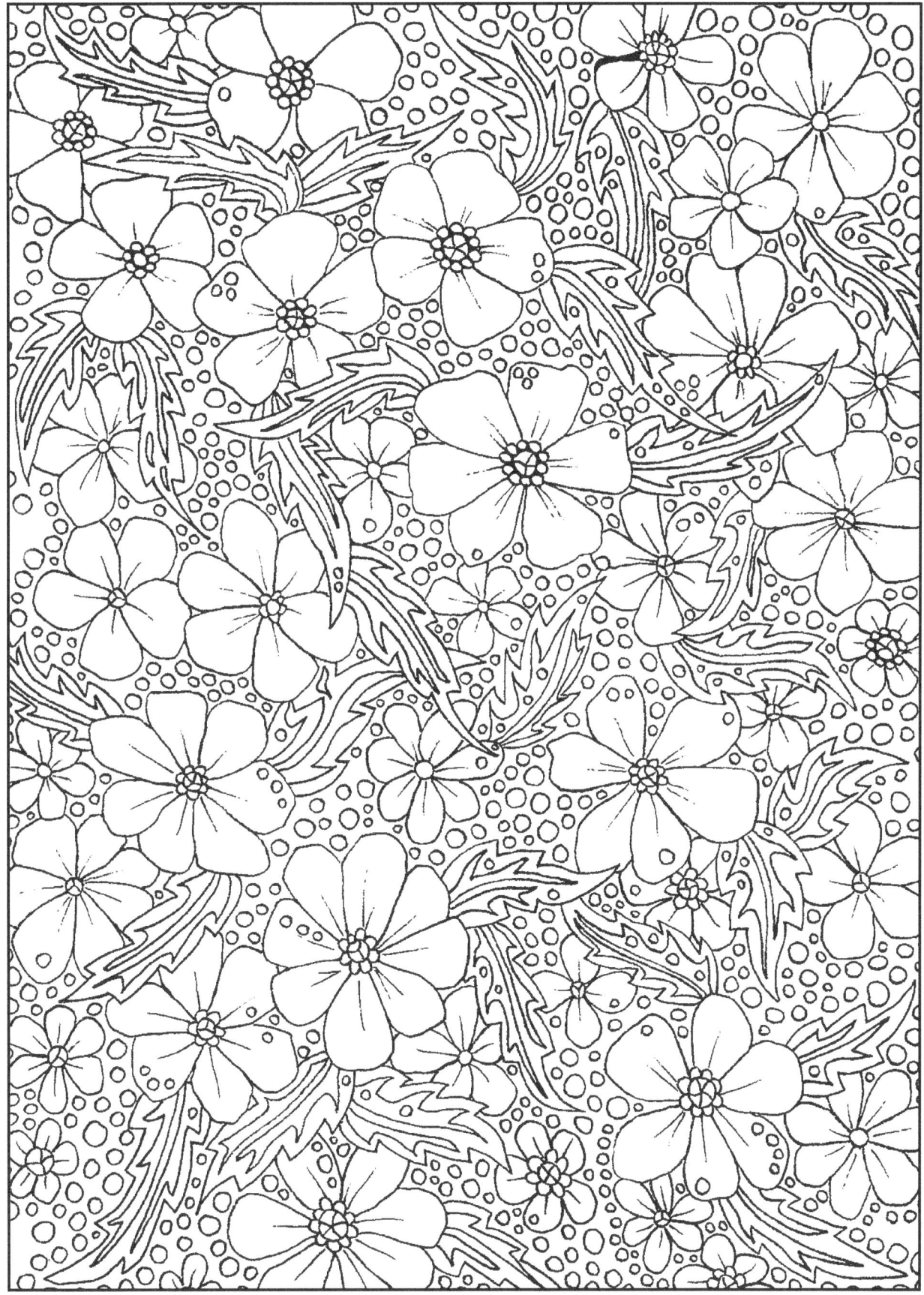

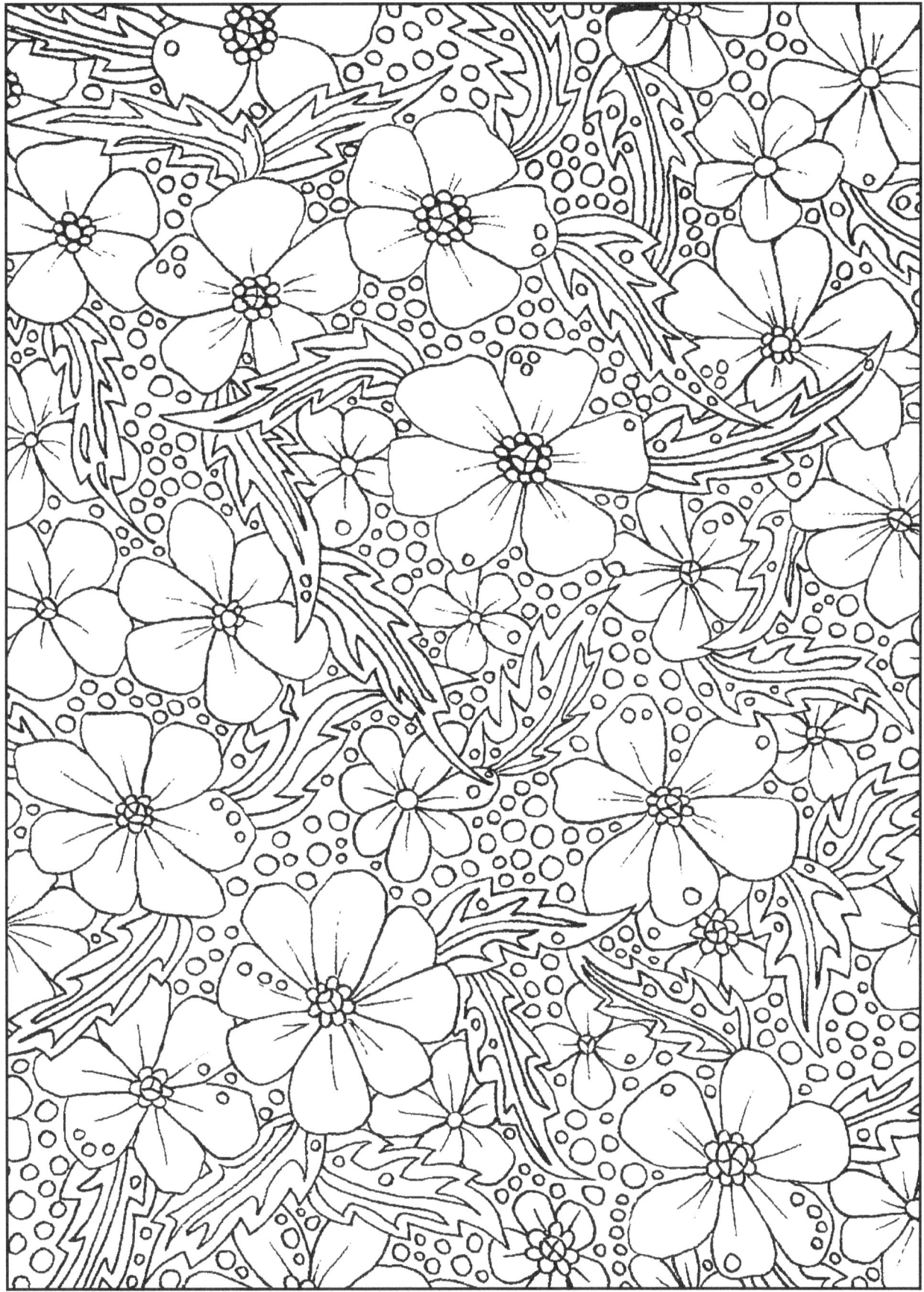

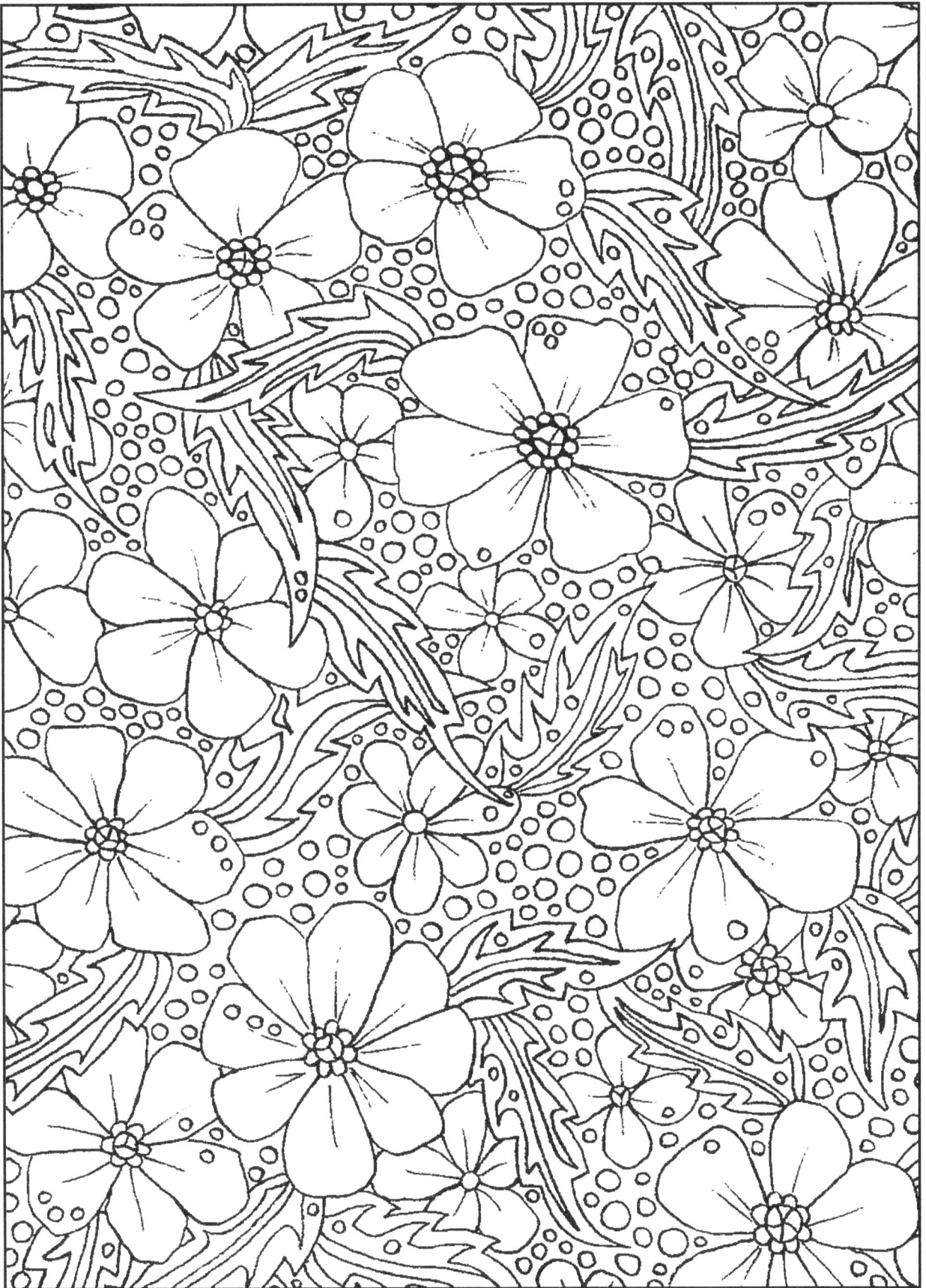

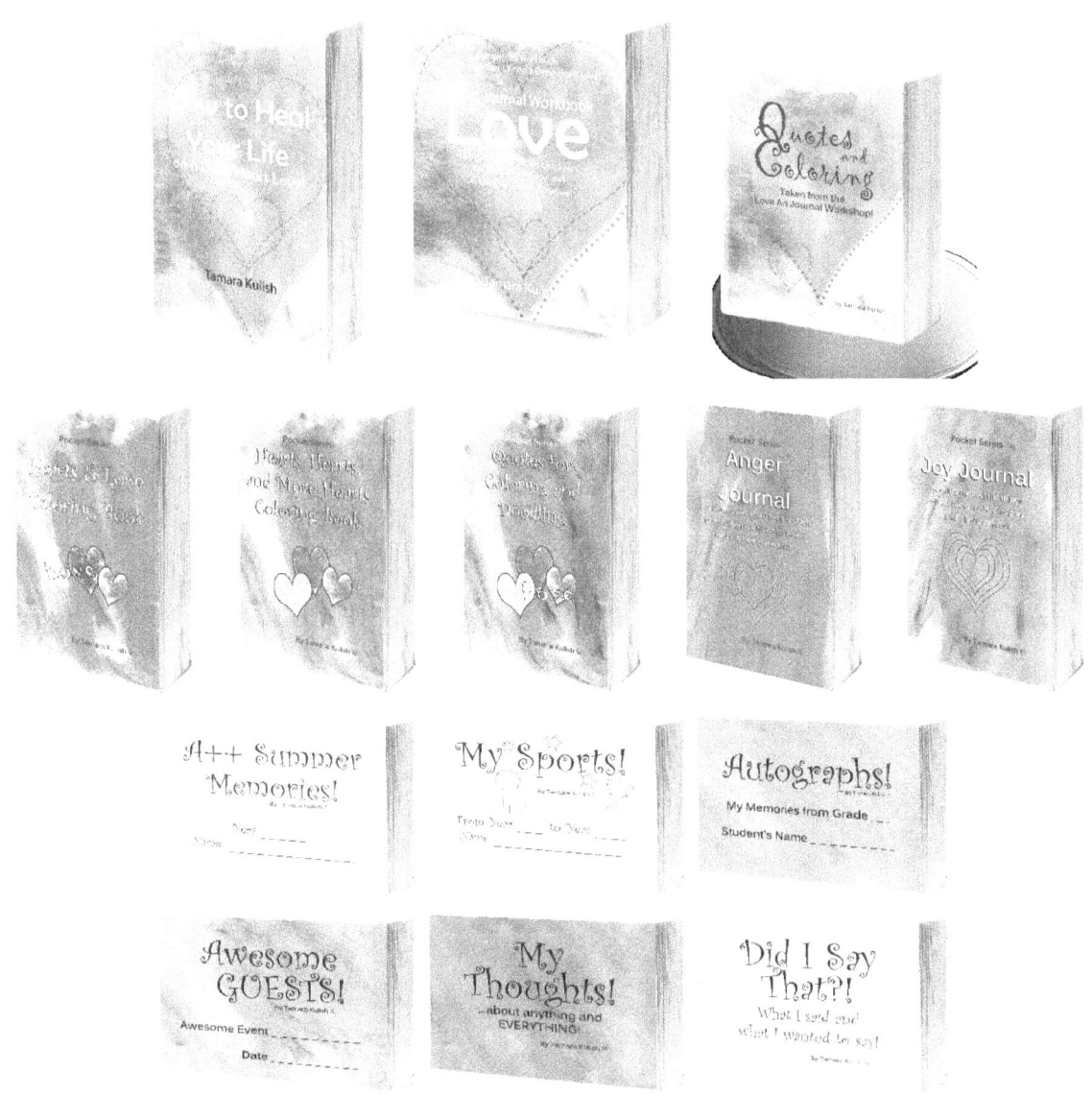

Thank you for buying
this book!

I hope you'll take the time to write a review... Other readers need to read your review!

www.ingramcontent.com/pod-product-compliance
Lightning Source LLC
Chambersburg PA
CBHW080833220526
45467CB00008B/2271